Traveling the World
Through Your Favorite Movies

FILM + TRAVEL

ASIA > OCEANIA > AFRICA

MUSEYON
GUIDES

A CURATED GUIDE TO YOUR OBSESSIONS

www.museyon.com

© Museyon, Inc. 2008

Publisher: Akira Chiba
Editor-in-Chief: Anne Ishii
Art Director: Alene Jackson
Production Manager: Michael Yong
Photography Editor: Michael Kuhle
Film Stills: Courtesy of Everett Collection

Permission to use *The Last Emperor* courtesy of: © Recorded Picture Company
Cover Illustration: © Jillian Tamaki copyright 2008

Published in the United States by:
Museyon, Inc.
20 E. 46th St. Ste. 1400
New York, NY 10017

Museyon is a registered trademark.
Visit us online at www.museyon.com

ISBN 978-0-9822320-1-9

021060

Printed in China

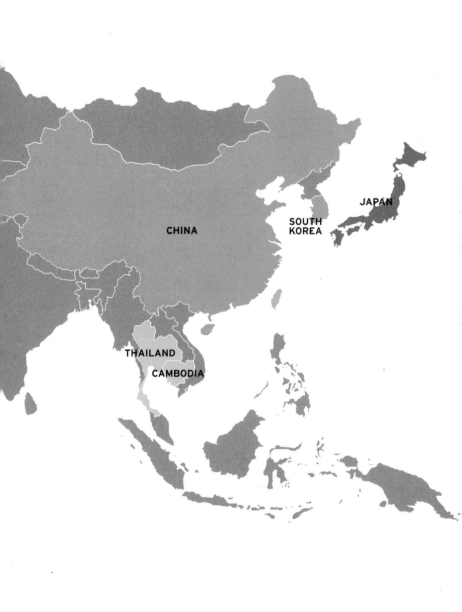

CHINA

JAPAN

SOUTH
KOREA

THAILAND

CAMBODIA

MAP : ASIA

AUSTRALIA

NEW ZEALAND

MAP : **OCEANIA**

MAP : **AFRICA**

TABLE OF CONTENTS

01 : HONG KONG NOCTURNE: THE CITY IN PICTURES   11

HONG KONG, CHINA BY SCARLET CHENG

02 : INSIDE AND BEYOND THE TOURIST TRAPS   27

SEOUL, SOUTH KOREA BY ELISE YOON

03 : A CINEMATIC CITY, OLD AND NEW   39

TOKYO, JAPAN BY EIJA NISKANEN

04 : THE EVERY WAR, THE EVERY EDEN   53

THAILAND + CAMBODIA BY JOSE LUSTRE JR.

05 : GREAT SOUTHERN FILMSCAPES 67
AUSTRALIA + NEW ZEALAND BY GEMMA BLACKWOOD

06 : BEYOND THE AXIS OF EVIL 85
IRAN BY MIKAEL AWAKE

07 : AN AMERICAN IN MOROCCO 99
MOROCCO BY JOSE LUSTRE JR.

08 : A LONG TIME AGO...FAR, FAR AWAY— 111
IN FILM
TUNISIA BY LEE MIDDLETON

TABLE OF CONTENTS

09 : BUILDING FANTASIES: EAST AFRICA IN FILM
EASTERN AFRICA BY LEE MIDDLETON

127

10 : KEEPING IT REAL IN SOUTHERN AFRICAN FILM
SOUTHERN AFRICA BY LEE MIDDLETON

141

READING / VIEWING
APPENDIX

155

INDEX + CREDITS
FILM

157

If I said "Asian Tourist," you would have an exact image in your head.

He's a skinny Japanese-looking man with a camera around his neck, surrounded by a flock of identical twins. The kind of guy who would be played by Gedde Watanabe, himself famous for playing Long Duk Dong in the John Hughes classic, *Sixteen Candles*. That stereotypical Asian has played pivotal roles in many a film. Where would *Crocodile Dundee* have been without the "Asian Tourists" in the New York City subway? What about *Gung Ho*? *Better Off Dead*? *Night Train*? Oh there are so many film tourists to learn from! Suffice it to say this stereotype has probably blind-sided many non-Asians from film-tourism in the East. And don't even get me started on African stereotypes in film! Think of all the safaris and jungle cruises we've missed out on simply because we think we've seen all the same movies.

That's why we created *The Museyon Guide: Film+Travel: Asia/Oceania/ Africa*. We have an award-winning Ethiopian-American film director taking us through Iran. An Asian-American journalist who's lived on the African continent longer than in the U.S., guiding us through southeastern Africa. A Finnish film professor showing us Tokyo...and all of them doing it, through the lens of film, for the sake of the new, intrepid traveler. The one who hates being called a tourist. The one who's ready to take that stereotypical Asian tourist's camera and shove it. We hope you enjoy it.

See you on location.

01

NOCTURNE: THE CITY IN PICTURES

HONG KONG, CHINA

SCARLET CHENG
Most memorable experience in film/travel: A set visit to Wong Kar-wai's *Ashes of Time* in remote Yulin, China, on the edge of the Gobi Desert. In that moment, modern China—both the technology of filmmaking and Wong's cinematic sensibilities—merged with the old.

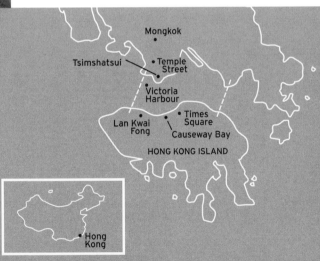

Mongkok

Tsimshatsui — Temple Street

Victoria Harbour

Lan Kwai Fong

Times Square

Causeway Bay

HONG KONG ISLAND

Hong Kong

Hong Kong is a dizzying patchwork of sleepy colonial past and vibrant capitalist present. In the shadow of gleaming glass and steel skyscrapers lies a rabbits' warren of streets, where cobblers mend shoes in tiny stalls while modern-day businessmen and women in Prada suits rush by, checking their iPhones. Add to the mix breathtaking views—from mountain peaks to undulating harbors—and you have the makings of a very photogenic city.

Moviemakers from around the world have long been drawn to the city's visual splendor, and despite its modest size, Hong Kong—now a Special Administrative Region under the People's Republic of China—has a powerhouse of a film industry. Foreign film companies first arrived in the 1950s, when location shooting and stories set in the exotic Far East were all the rage in Hollywood. Films from these early days included both comedies like *The Road to Hong Kong* (1962) and melodramas like *Love is a Many-Splendored Thing* (1955) and *The World of Suzie Wong* (1960).

In the 1990s, the territory produced over 200 films a year. Many were shot on location, making use of winding old roads and sleek modern freeways, dilapidated tenements and soaring mansions, smoky temples and state-of-the-art shopping malls. Some—especially action films like those by John Woo, Kirk Wong and Johnny To—found avid audiences abroad.

These days it seems the skyscrapers have taken over. In the last ten years, a host of old buildings has been torn down, parts of Victoria Harbour filled in, and a whole crop of new buildings raised up. But the old persists. Even off busy Queen's Road, a block or two from the subway, sidewalk stalls still line the alleys, selling clothing and household items; old-style cafes and noodle shops are tucked in amongst the trendy coffee shops and boutiques. So it

14

makes sense to start a tour with a couple of wonderfully old and scenic ways to get about the city: the ferry and the tram.

HONG KONG FERRY

There's a delicious moment in *The World of Suzie Wong* when Robert Lomax (William Holden) first meets the saucy Suzie (Nancy Kwan). She jumps up from her seat on the Star Ferry when he begins to stare at her. Just arrived from the United States, he's a budding artist and wants to draw her picture. But when he approaches, she barks, "No talk!" That's because she's a very proper young Chinese lady, she says, who cannot speak to strangers. Later, in Wanchai, a dodgy working-class area of old Hong Kong, he finds out the truth: she's a lady of the night.

The Hong Kong Ferry goes from the tip of Tsimshatsui—on the tip of Kowloon Peninsula across Victoria Harbour from Hong Kong Island—to the Central and Wanchai areas of the city. This is a cheap way to get across the harbor—and wonderfully scenic, as well. Pay in advance and go to the waiting area, but note that boarding and disembarking happen very quickly; during rush hour you may get pushed along in the crowd. (Here, as in other crowded places, mind your personal belongings!) Or try taking the trip in the evening, when this city of skyscrapers is lit up like a diadem at the edge of the dark churning waters.

THE TRAM

The double-decker tram is another of Hong Kong's readily available sight-seeing opportunities, and a bargain to boot—it's only HK$2 for a ride from end to end. Pay exact change or swipe your pre-loaded Octopus card on your way out. Trams go slowly, stopping frequently, and run through the main arteries of congested downtown. Some are headed to Kennedy Town on the western end of Hong Kong island, and to Shau Kei Wan on the eastern end. Others veer off at Causeway Bay toward Happy Valley, one of the two major racetracks in gambling-happy Hong Kong. On race days, these trolleys are packed to the gills with working-class folk on their way to the tracks; the moneyed take the taxi or private car.

The trolley has figured in a number of Hong Kong films—including one of my favorites, *Rouge* (1987), directed by Stanley Kwan and starring the haunting Anita Mui as a prewar courtesan who returns to modern Hong Kong in search

‹ [top] **Star Ferry** photo: ©Richard Moross
[bottom] **Hong Kong Tram** photo: ©Satbir Sing

of her long-lost lover. It's a love story, it's a ghost story, but most of all it's a story about the passing of time and the changes in the city—some good, some not so good. In one memorable sequence, the protagonist gets on a tram, thinking he's alone on the upper deck, when a strange woman (Mui) appears out of nowhere. When he realizes that she's a ghost, he's terrified.

TSIMSHATSUI

Chungking Express (1994) was many foreigners' first exposure to auteur Wong Kar-wai. It was his third film, and his first truly international one—distributed in the United States by Quentin Tarantino's own Rolling Thunder Pictures. The film is an offbeat romantic comedy in two parts, both about lovelorn cops. Much of part one is set around **Chungking Mansions** (36 - 44 Nathan Road), a block-long building in busy Tsimshatsui that's known for its eclectic mix of restaurants, shops, restaurants and some very cheap hotels and long-term residences.

In *Chungking Express*, He Zhiwu (Takeshi Kaneshiro) is a plainclothes cop slowly coming to grips with the fact that his girlfriend has dumped him. He befriends a blond-wigged woman (Brigitte Lin) at a bar, but unbeknownst to him, she's a gangster having a bad day. She had recruited several Indians from Chungking Mansions as drug runners—but they disappeared on her at Kai Tak Airport (now defunct). Wong's follow-up to *Chungking Express* was *Fallen Angels* (1998), which also starred Kaneshiro, this time as young man who lives with his father in a Chungking Mansions rooming house.

Parts of the Hong Kong films *Comrades, Almost a Love Story* (1996) and *Infernal Affairs* (2002), were shot in the area around Tsimshatsui and adjoining **Mongkok** (see below). And the James Bond flick *The Man with the Golden Gun* (1974) features a scene in which Bond (Roger Moore) walks up to the **Peninsula Hotel**, the last of several legendary old Hong Kong hotels. Though extensively renovated, it retains a grand lobby, which is a marvelous place

^ ***The Man with the Golden Gun,*** 1974. photo: ©Everett Collection
> **Mongkok at night** photo: ©Ernesto Andrade

兆萬飲食 物中心

CTMA CENTRE

FASHION MARK 時裝廣場

for drinks or afternoon tea. Later, lying in wait for the villain, Bond lurks outside the infamous **Bottoms Up**, a girlie bar located in Tsimshatsui at the time of filming; in 2004 it relocated to Wanchai.

Just north of Tsimshatsui is Mongkok, home to **Temple Street** and its famous night market of hawkers, fortune-tellers and sidewalk singers. The market features in the romantic comedy *C'est La Vie, Mon Cherie*, a sentimental favorite when released in 1993. Here, romantic lead Lau Ching Wan gets his fortune told and Anita Yuen, playing his perky love, and her family perform Cantonese opera.

VICTORIA HARBOUR/CENTRAL
Victoria Harbour is the body of water dividing mountainous Hong Kong Island from Tsimshatsui. The harbor and its beautiful coastlines have been seen in many films, from the opening sequences of *Love is a Many-Splendored Thing* (1955), which starred Jennifer Jones as a Eurasian doctor, to the action-packed police thriller *Rush Hour* (1998), starring Jackie Chan as a detective. The former highlights quaint go-downs (warehouses), buildings constructed in stately British-colonial style, and even a port filled with junk—all hard to find nowadays. *Rush Hour*, on the other hand, presents modern Hong Kong—including a glittering, panoramic nighttime view of the Central and Wanchai from the water.

Lara Croft Tomb Raider: The Cradle of Life (2003) also showcases the skyline, as the villain (played by Ciaran Hinds) lands his plane at a (nonexistent) private airport. Director Jan de Bont remembers landing at the old Kai Tak Airport in Kowloon. "It was quite exciting, landing between the high-rise buildings," he once said, "and that's what I kinda had in mind—to recreate that a little bit." In that shot one of the most identifiable buildings is the **Bank of China Tower** (1 Garden Road) designed by renowned architect I. M. Pei, whose design was inspired by tall and resilient bamboo. Opened in 1990, the 70-story building is faced with tinted glass divided by braces in a triangular pattern. For a few years it was the tallest building in Hong Kong, before—in this ever-ambitious city—it was bested by one still taller. Still, it's worth visiting the observation deck on the 43rd floor, which affords a fine view of the harbor.

The Art Deco **Bank of China**, a solid and stately old building (2 A Des Voeux Road), is nearby. The China Club, the private restaurant and club

< **Mirador Mansions, Tsim Sha Tsui** photo: ©Germain Meyer

founded by David Tang (who also founded the Shanghai Tang stores) is at the top. You can take the elevator up and look around the lobby, with its quaint Shanghai-deco interior and avant-garde Chinese paintings, or if you know a member, go inside and enjoy some of the best dim sum the city has to offer.

Another scene in *Lara Croft* shows the fearless heroine (played by Angelina Jolie) jumping from the 83rd story of the **International Finance Centre** on Harbour View Street—specially Two IFC, the tallest building in Hong Kong. At the time *Lara Croft* was filmed, it was under construction, but the latest installment in the Batman franchise, *The Dark Knight* (2008), also makes use of Central's skyline and skyscrapers—and a completed IFC. In a breathtaking leap from Two IFC to One IFC, Batman, having tracked a villain from Gotham to Hong Kong, smashes through the glass exterior into an office to capture his prey. The real complex includes offices and a lively shopping concourse on lower levels.

LAN KWAI FONG

Both cops in *Chungking Express* patronize a small carryout, the Midnight Express, on Lan Kwai

ON LOCATION WITH ZHANG YIMOU

Takeshi Kaneshiro was late. Again.

It was December 2003 and we were on the set of *House of Flying Daggers*, Chinese movie (and now, Olympics) director Zhang Yimou's follow-up to the wildly successful *Hero*, which had outperformed even *Titanic* at the mainland Chinese box office. As they had been for the last week or so, the crew was hard at work shooting the justly famous bamboo forest action scene in a nature preserve in **Yongchuan County**, approximately an hour's drive from the city of **Chongqing** in Sichuan Province.

Kaneshiro, the half-Japanese, half-Taiwanese heartthrob best known in America for his turn as a love-struck young cop in Wong Kar-wai's *Chungking Express*, had managed to make himself extremely unpopular on the set by virtue of a work ethic somewhere between that of a wayward puppy dog and … a love-struck young cop. Nobody could figure out why it always took him so long to come out of his trailer. Maybe he was too busy checking the expiration dates on pineapple cans.

There are, contrary to popular belief, few places in the world as boring as a film set. Long stretches of tedium with nothing to do are punctuated by mere moments of "action." This is doubly true of the set for a film that involves a lot of CGI, because the time involved getting the technical details right grows exponentially, and because you have to "imagine" what the final result is going to look like. And it's trebly true of a film set at which one of the two main stars hasn't shown up yet.

‹ **International Finance Centre** photo: ©Cristina Ciochina

21

So, with nothing better to do, my companion and I began to wander around. There's something particularly magical about the sunlight in a bamboo forest. Bamboo trees are narrow enough, and their leaves sparse enough, that much of the sunlight passes through unimpeded—yet at the same time it's reflected and refracted into a kind of murky green. After walking awhile, we emerged onto a trail along the side of the mountain, from which we could see the bamboo trees below us swaying in the wind, as well as the industrial smog from a city nearby.

In due course we grew tired of all the walking and headed back to the set. Kaneshiro had finally arrived, and the crew was busy preparing a shot that would take an hour to shoot and last all of about two seconds on the screen. My companion and I found some seats. We followed what was happening on set for a time, but our interest quickly waned, at which point we cracked out some books and started reading.

After a particularly exasperating take, Director Zhang looked over and noticed us with the books in our hands. "You two are lucky," he said, almost wistfully. "You're actually learning something, cultivating your minds. Me, I'm just over here cranking out entertainment."

(Courtesy of Kerim Yasar)

Fong, a popular restaurant and club street just above Central. The name is also given to the area formed by the intersections of Lan Kwai Fong, D'Aguilar, and Wyndham Street. In *Rush Hour 2* (2001) there's an exterior shot of a nightclub there.

In part two of *Chungking*, the uniformed Cop 663 (Tony Leung) meets with Faye (Faye Wong), who works behind the counter of the Midnight Express—but alas, the place no longer exists. It's now a 7-11! The whole area, in fact, has gotten quite gentrified of late, and is now full of expensive boutiques and upmarket bars. Still, it's a lively nightspot, attracting Hong Kong yuppies and Westerners alike.

TIMES SQUARE/ CAUSEWAY BAY

Causeway Bay is a busy shopping and restaurant area popular with middle-class families and the young, although with the creation of the swank **Times Square** it's gotten downright hip. In *Lara Croft Tomb Raider: The Cradle of Life* (2003) Lara and her partner-in-adventure Terry Sheridan (Gerard Butler) find themselves in the plaza of Times Square. As pedestrians swirl around them, they attempt to locate a special

> ^ *House of Flying Daggers*, 2004. photo: ©Sony Pictures Classics/Everett Collection
> > **Star Ferry** photo: ©Sam D Cruz

orb, which is in the possession of the villain whose lair lies in the building before them. The real Times Square offers 14 floors of shops and restaurants; the gourmet CitySuper market in the basement purveys delectable imports from Japan, Europe and the U. S., including a nice selection of wines. On the same level there are also a number of good fast-food vendors and a common seating area.

In *Revenge of the Pink Panther* (1978), the notorious Inspector Clouseau (Peter Sellers) goes to Hong Kong in pursuit of a mafia boss. He lands at Kai Tak Airport and checks into **The Excelsior Hotel**, situated right near the **Hong Kong Yacht Club** and the **Noon Day Gun**, which fires every day at noon, according to a long tradition. In *Die Another Day* (2002) James Bond (Pierce Brosnan) escapes captivity and jumps off a ship into Hong Kong Harbour, emerging at the Yacht Club. Alert viewers will note that, since the high-rises of Hong Kong Island are visible across the waters, it can't be the actual Yacht Club—but that's movie reality for you!

Here, as across Hong Kong, one can find the old amidst the new. For a vintage experience, visit the **Goldfinch Restaurant** (13 - 15 Lan Fong Road), which serves Hong Kong-style Western food like pepper steak and borscht. This dimly lit eatery still evokes the 1960s, when it first opened. No wonder Wong Kar-wai had the would-be lovers of *In the Mood for Love* (2000), played by Maggie Cheung and Tony Leong, meeting there. §

Scarlet Cheng is a life-long film aficionado. She has an M.A. in Film Studies from the University of Maryland, College Park, then REALLY learned how film was made when she lived in Hong Kong in the 1990s. There she met and interviewed directors, costume designers and of course actors and actresses working in China, Hong Kong and Taiwan – sometimes on studio sets and on location. She has written for many publications, including the *Los Angeles Times*, *New York Times*, *Premiere*, *Village Voice* and *Vogue*, and currently teaches film history at two colleges in the Los Angeles area.

C1 호야상회
T.246-2472
C1 충무상회
T.246-0932
C1 근실상회
C1 신평상회
T.245-7921
C1 복영상회

02

INSIDE AND BEYOND THE TOURIST TRAPS
SEOUL, SOUTH KOREA

ELISE YOON
Most memorable experience in film/travel: Visiting the Great Wall of China near Beijing. It was incredible to see what humans were capable of.

A discussion of contemporary Korean cinema would be incomplete without mention of filmmakers like Park Chan-wook and Bong Joon-ho, just as a tourist's trip to Seoul would be empty without a walk along the Han River or a meal at a *budae jigae jip* (restaurant specializing in "army trash stew"). The works of contemporary directors such as Park and Bong have been lauded by the most discriminating of international critics, but also widely viewed by Korean theatergoers, and they all share a clear and realistic shot of Seoul's most recognized elements.

What makes the global acceptance and praise of these filmmakers particularly poignant though, is its taking place despite what until recently were considered commercially unbreakable cultural barriers. Until the 2000s, many of the Seoul locations I will mention here would only have been interesting to native residents.

Park Chan-wook, in particular, has hit a chord with international and domestic audiences since the release of his "Vengeance" trilogy—*Sympathy*

for Mr. Vengeance (2002), *Oldboy* (2003), *Sympathy for Lady Vengeance* (2005)—which blurs distinctions between good and evil into a wild and highly stylized mess. By making gruesome plot points like incest and torture a prerequisite for satisfying conclusion, he forces us to question our system of ethics and morals—to question our entire belief system.

Bong Joon-ho's *The Host* was a surprise hit in the U.S., considering the decidedly anti-American plot element that sets the whole movie in motion: said oppressor nation is responsible for the birth of the film's titular "host" (a yonic CGI phantasm of a monster, measuring at least ten yards in length). Since starring in *The Host*, it's its lead actor Kang-ho Song has experienced

⌃ **Sympathy for Mr. Vengeance,** 2005. photo: ©Tartan Films/Everett Collection
‹ **Yukkae Jang Stew** photo: ©L.W. Yang

Hollywood-level celebrity status, something of a relatively new boon to the burgeoning film mega-industry of the peninsula. But it is not hard to understand why Song is a favorite of Korea's top directors; he easily plays villain or hero and has the ability to inject humor to the most serious of roles.

Kang Je-gyu's *Taegugki* ("Brotherhood of War" 2004) was a major block-buster long on the heels of *Shiri* ("Shiri" 1999), which had catapulted at least one of its all-star cast members (Kim Yunjin) into American cult status when she joined the cast of its hit television show, *Lost*, as Sun Kwon opposite her small screen husband Daniel Dae Kim.

Unlike their Hollywood counterparts, Korean filmmakers have little physical space to hold soundstages or large studios for shooting. But Korea itself, with its constantly changing landscape, has by default become an ideal movie setting. Here are a handful of visit-worthy sites within easy reach of any tourist's first jaunt to the country.

For the real die-hard film fanatic, a trip to the only production facility on a scale measuring to Hollywood will be worth the short bus trip. The **KOFIC (Korean Film Council) Studio** houses the largest film production facilities in Asia, and is located just outside of Seoul in the city of Namyangju. Away from the noise and smog of Seoul, the studios include several major outdoor sets, including a recreated version of the Joint Security Area at the North-South Korean demilitarized zone—built for the film *J.S.A.* (2000) directed by Park Chan-wook.

In the studio lot are also two medieval Korean villages and a Choson Dynasty-era palace that has been used and reused in several historical films including *Chihwaseon* (2002) by contemporary Korean cinema godfather Im Kwon-taek; *Untold Scandal* (2002) by Lee Je-yong, based on *Dangerous Liaisons*; and *King and the Clown* (2005) by Lee Jun-ik. The indoor facilities include sound studios, several exhibitions—including one dedicated to Korean film history—and a costume and prop storage area that are open to the public at around $3 a pop.

For obvious reasons, director Park Chan-wook could not film *J.S.A.* at the real **joint security area** that protects South Korea from the Democratic People's Republic of Korea. What many do not know is that non-Korean citizens may visit the **DMZ** (Demilitarized Zone) in guided tours at any time. Herein lies

⟨ **View of Han River** photo: ©grafica

one major exception to the modern adventuresome tourist's reluctance to fall in line with a pre-packaged destination trip on a chartered bus, as it is a luxury unknown to the neighboring residents. The DMZ is about an hour and a half drive from Seoul and tours typically include a quick history lesson, a walk through a tunnel dug by North Koreans, a view of the DPRK's "Propaganda Village" ghost town, as well as the Joint Security Area. Originally built at the end of the Korean War for temporary usage, simple blue buildings still stand, marking the border between the two Koreas.

MAJOR HANGOUTS

Meanwhile, back in the capital, **Han River** runs east and west through Seoul and serves as the backdrop for the Korean monster movie, *The Host*. Those who have seen other films by director Bong Joon-ho, such as *Barking Dogs*

Never Bite (2000) or *Memories of Murder* (2003) know to expect more than just a horror flick, however. Song Kang-ho stars as Dang-gu, a slacker-father who is just barely manning his food stand on the riverside park when a monster emerges from the polluted waters and kidnaps his daughter. Dang-gu and his Olympic archer sister (archery being, incidentally, an Olympic sport totally dominated by Koreans), go in hot pursuit of the American kidnapper-monster.

Though the park extends all along the banks of the river through several districts, the park on **Yeouido Island** is the most popular spot. Nearby, the Han Gang Sewer was used in actual shooting for the film's dirtier sewer scenes. The use of the heart of Seoul itself as a filming location heightens the surrealism of the story, as a digital monster is inserted into a scene visible to everyday Seoul passersby. Food stands like the one in the movie dot the entire Korean capital, but as suggested in the film, the Han River waters are not ideal for recreational swimming.

Kang Je-gyu's 1999 Korean blockbuster *Shiri*, as well as the Hong Kong film *Seoul Raiders* (2005), both set high-speed adrenaline-fueled climaxes at

^ *The Host*, 2006. photo: ©Magnolia Pictures/Everett Collection
> [top] **Han River Bridge trellis shot in** *The Host* photo: ©Peter Verkovensky
[bottom] **Tunnel, DMZ** photo: ©Ville Miettinen

Olympic Stadium. It's no wonder, as a sporting arena already lends itself to racing heartbeats. In *Shiri's* final scenes, North Korean spies are plotting to blow up the stadium while the South Korean president is attending a soccer game between the two Koreas. Though the story of *Seoul Raiders* is not as integral to the location, shots allow one to see the curving rim characteristic of the stadium, modeled after traditional Korean pottery. Built for the 1988 Seoul Summer Olympic Games, the stadium is part of the massive **Jamsil Sports Complex** and still hosts sell-out standing-room-only athletic events and concerts.

In *Sympathy For Mr. Vengeance*, the first in Park Chan-wook's "Vengeance Trilogy," Song Kang-ho plays the single father of a kidnapped girl. Following ransom instructions, he takes the subway and a small *ma-ul* bus (a local green line with very short routes) to the top of **Geumho Mountain**. The tennis court, playground, hiking trail and pavilion are all totally isolated, and make for a nice day of quiet recreation for the more active traveler, but the view in and of itself would make going there worth it. It is from the sports courtside overlooking Seoul that Song nervously waits for the captors, clutching a case of ransom money.

While Park is a fixture in Korean cinema thanks to a commanding first career as a film critic, and though he is native to and concerned with the capital city and its local culture, he has also shot in **Pusan**, along with many other domestic and international directors. The south seaside port is a popular tourist destination, and the home of one of Asia's biggest film festivals, but the metropol has become a popular filming location of late, thanks to the Busan Film Commission (sic) and various tax shelters that have been provided for prospective filmmakers. If you have a weekend to explore the city alleys featured in *Old Boy* (2003) or Kwak Kyung-taek's *Friend* (2001), you have but to board a high-speed train from Seoul down to Pusan. The trip is around four hours long, but rolls through a side of Korea rarely seen on film.

The second installment in the "Vengeance" series, *Sympathy for Lady Vengeance*, centers around Geum-ja, a beautiful woman who has just finished her jail sentence for murder. However the circumstances of her crime beg our inquiry. Geum-ja has allegedly murdered an unrelated four year-old boy, herself but a young woman. Having to leave a suspicious husband to care for their precocious daughter, Park invariably takes us through another wild

〈 [top] **Pusan**
[bottom] **Pusan Street** photos: ©L.W. Yang

examination of morality. In one pivotal scene in the back story, families and students are gathered at an aquarium on a field trip. The teenage Geum-ja, still in her high school uniform, reveals she is pregnant. Located in the **COEX Mall**, the aquarium is the largest in Korea and boasts over 600 species of marine life.

Much later in the film after Geum-ja has reestablished a life for herself out of the slammer, she takes up French pastry baking, and is hired by a ubiquitous chain of bakeries in Seoul called **Tous Les Jours**. The particular outlet she worked in is located in a suburb northeast of Seoul called Ilsan (take the 3 train to the Baeksok stop), but the beautiful cakes shot on film can be purchased at any of Tous Les Jours' several metropolitan outposts. In fact, the film did such a good job of advertising the precious cakes that cooking schools now offer courses specifically on how to recreate these edible gems.

MY SASSY SEOUL

The 2001 hit romantic comedy *My Sassy Girl* centers around Kyun-woo, a young man who falls in love with a girl despite her wild behavior and all the horrifying grief she makes him suffer. For the girl's birthday (who remains anonymous throughout the film), Kyun-woo plans a surprise trip to **Seoul Land Amusement Park** after hours. The date takes an unexpected turn when the two bump into an AWOL soldier who takes them hostage. Kyun-woo's vision of romantic fireworks turns sour when the soldier threatens to start taking lives and the military gets involved.

After a long day at the amusement park, get yourself to **Jjul Bying Budae Jigae** in the hip college-student ward of Sinchon, where the thoroughly abused Kyun-woo and his sassy pain-in-the-butt girlfriend sup. Be sure to order the only thing on their menu: budae jigae (army trash stew), so named because Koreans under the occupation would gather what G.I.s let to waste, and throw it into a pot of spicy ramyun. §

Elise Jongeun Yoon is a Korean-American currently studying telecommunications. Her hobbies include music, watching movies, photography and travel.

03

A CINEMATIC CITY, OLD AND NEW

TOKYO, JAPAN

EIJA NISKANEN
Most memorable experience in film/travel: Traveling through Japan with a Japan Rail Pass and seeing many of the castles Akira Kurosawa shot in his films.

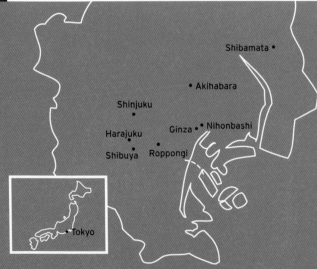

Shibamata •

• Akihabara

Shinjuku
•

Ginza • Nihonbashi
Harajuku •
•
Shibuya Roppongi

• Tokyo

Tokyo is a city made immemorial by Godzilla, that sympathetic monster-lizard of Japanese popular cinema. The modern image of Tokyo filled with high-rises begging to be crushed by such monsters, has been featured in many films since The War, both Japanese and foreign. Influences of this postmodern, science-fiction look-alike city have been filtered through the setup of such dystopic futurisms as *Blade Runner*, which was in turn a hidden homage to Los Angeles. Tokyo, however, still possesses the remains of a different kind of shabbier, cozier town. The exact charm of Tokyo is in this side-by-side existence of the ultramodern and the traditional past.

The Showa era (1926-89, named after Emperor Hirohito) has been a popular target of nostalgic imagination in Japanese popular media, including in movies, such as *ALWAYS—Sunset on Third Street* (2005) and its sequel (2007). **Tokyo Tower**, that quintessential postcard icon, was built in 1958, when the film was set, and serves as an anchor for the era in question. The tower's surrounding neighborhood, outlined by homely narrow streets filled with mom-and-pop businesses that may be a disappearing feature, will survive at least in celluloid, amidst the hectic urban development that seems to be a permanent characteristic of the city.

Nostalgia for traditional Tokyo actually started during the last decades of the Showa era itself, as this urban development threw the remnants of traditional neighborhoods further away from central Tokyo. But during the 1990s and into the turn of the millennium, contemporary youth and otaku (subculture fanatics) culture has also been featured in film, staged in the epicenters of youth paradise: Shibuya, Harajuku and Akihabara. Here we have to add the postmodern Tokyo as seen through the eyes of foreign filmmakers such as Sofia Coppola.

Although Tokyo cannot boast a landscape of such historically Japanese iconography as the magnificent ancient temples and palaces of Kyoto, there are areas that possess an antiquated shabby post-war homeliness. As you walk along **Ginza** and the old **Nihonbashi** area (both featured in Edo period woodblock prints), you can almost visualize bygone caravans of merchants moving along the Todaido pass to sell their wares at what is now

‹ **Tokyo Tower** photo: ©Hannahmaria

the Daimaru department store basin. You'll see signs for precious little watering holes, and mama-sans—a non-sexualized bar equivalent of a "madame"—hurrying to their bars, getting ready for another busy evening. Yasujiro Ozu's movies, like *Equinox Flower* (1958), depict this 1950s and early-1960s Nihonbashi, in the wake of Japan's recovery from war destruction; a neighborhood busy building its economy. Central to this economy were salarymen, or white-collar workers, who kept burgeoning companies on the up and up. After a busy day at work they stopped by bars with names like Luna, which in *Equinox Flower* was where Joe Salaryman would unravel to a bevy of waitresses, mama-sans and hostesses sympathetically listening. These bars still exist in the tributary alleys off Ginza, their signs lighting up in the twilight, under weeping willows dotting the streets.

Ozu had a talent for making the shabby, unplanned construction, and crisscrossing public utilities wires look poetic, and even humorous. His bar interiors have a minimal cool look, with bottles lined up neatly behind an ever-polite bartender. Take a look through any narrow alley and focus out to the passersby at the other end—an instant Ozu shot. If you take a photo from ground level, you have yourself a replica of Ozu's iconic film angles.

TORA-SAN RETURNS HOME TO SHIBAMATA

Another kind of nostalgia for the traditional lives in the *Otoko wa tsurai yo* (It's Tough Being a Man) a.k.a. Tora-san film series, the longest running movie series ever, with 48 movies made between 1969-95. The main protagonist, Tora-san, is an over-optimistic, clumsily charming, wandering street peddler of random sundry goods.

To get a cinematic look at the entirety of Japan, you need look no further than what is familiarly called "The Tora-san movies." In each film, Tora-san visits a new hidden gem of a Japanese region. He usually meets a woman there, collectively referred to as Tora-san's Madonnas, each played by a famous actress. However after every trip out into the beautiful countryside,

ˆ *Early Summer,* 1951. photo: ©Everett Collection
‹ **Night Alley, Nihonbashi, Old Tokyo** photo: ©Toshihiro Oimatsu

Tora-san returns home to downtown Tokyo, and re-encounters the Madonna, invariably there to briefly escape home. Tora-san always falls in love with the woman, who always has some man waiting somewhere in the background. Hilarity and hassle follow. Finally, Tora-san—again contemplating his sad fate (hence the film series title)—hits the road anew.

In every opening credit sequence, we see Tora-san's native hood of **Shibamata**, in the Katsushika borough, situated in the eastern working-class neighborhood of Tokyo. Take the Keisei train line to Shibamata, and you'll see Tora-san painted on the train cars. The train gets to the same station from which Tora-san left so many times for his travels. On the station square, take a picture with the Tora-san statue. From there you can stroll through the *shotengai*, or shopping promenade, toward the local temple. Along the street are traditional sweets shops, identical to the one Tora-san's relatives run in the movie series. In the front you can buy traditional snacks such as *kusa-dango* (grass-based mochi sweet) and *shio-senbei* (salty rice crackers). You can take a break and have your tea and sweets in the shop's tables in the rear, served by friendly staff in ubiquitous white uniforms. In between the sweet shops and restaurant are souvenir shops, which feature many Tora-san-themed gifts. There is, of course, also a Tora-san museum.

Once you're through the promenade, you'll find yourself in the **Taishakuten Temple** quarters. This is where Tora-san's sister, the protective Sakura, spills her concerns over Tora-san's naive behavior. Her proxy therapist is Gozen-sama, the priest of the temple, who was played by the very same Ryu Chishu who so memorably played the father-salaryman figure in most of Ozu's films. The head groundskeeper in the film series is one Genkou, Tora-san's foolish best friend. The temple was built in 1629 and its main building is covered by an interesting wood carving, depicting animals of Buddhist lore over three strata—uppermost being the home of flying animals, the center level covered in earth and its land-bound animals in familiar religious scenes, and the lowest featuring sea and water animals.

A BUBBLY, TRENDY TOWN

Another moment of clear interpretation in film is Japan during its "bubble economy." The name seems inappropriately cheery in light of the country's subsequent bubble popping and international financial crisis, but during the late 1980s, the Nikkei index (Japanese stock market) shot way up. The yen was a respected currency, and Japanese companies were shopping

American real estate. The epicenter of this economy bolstered by brand new credit cards, was **Roppongi**, which to this day renowned as a foreigner-frequented nightlife spot.

Roppongi of the bygone bubble economy and its later demise are both featured in the recent comedy film *Bubble Fiction: Boom or Bust* (2007). The movie's main character, a young bubble-headed woman named Mayumi, is trying to pay off her vanished ex-boyfriend's huge debt by working as a hostess in a club. Assigned by the Finance Ministry to go back to March, 1990 with a time machine, she's been ordered to prevent the bursting of the bubble. The bygone Roppongi and Akasaka neighborhoods make for a hilarious send-up on fashion that feels almost ancient in hindsight: "body-con" dresses, one-length hair and thick eyebrows. This was the era of "big disco," since replaced by seedier small *gaijin* (primarily American foreigners) bars by the late 1990s. The latter 1990s post-bubble era is best captured by Takashi Ishii in his gangster movie *Gonin* (1995), in which a disco owner, having ended up in debt for the Japanese mob, or yakuza (clearly a recurring theme), organizes a team of five men to rob the mob's stash. The post-bubble era witnessed the transformation of Roppongi from mainstream trendy to a sort of low-rent red-light district catering to foreigners.

More recently, the city has consciously organized the renaissance of Roppongi, hoping to mutate it back into a major shopping, leisure and

artistic center. Every October, **Roppongi Hills**, a multilevel shopping, restaurant and entertainment mall, hosts Japan's biggest film event, the Tokyo International Film Festival, in its Virgin-Toho multiplex. The same complex houses the **Mori Art Museum**, which has exhibited some of the most critically lauded modern art in Tokyo. From the museum's **Sky View Deck** you have a marvelous view over Tokyo.

So where do the fashionable youngsters go? Of course to **Shibuya**, that mecca for hip young adults. This is where they start when visiting Tokyo from their small-town Japan. Like any crowded and popular neighborhood, Shibuya has its seedy underbelly too. A bevy of love hotels on the **Dogenzaka**, for example, are a popular outpost for more recent movies about teenage girls in tawdry *enjo kosai* relationship (euphemistically translating as "compensation dating") with middle-aged men. A clear look at this practice is captured in Masato Harada's *Bounce-Ko-gals* (1997) and *Evangelion* (1995)-creator Hideaki Anno's live action film *Love & Pop* (1998). But *Shibu*, Shibuya in teenage slang, is not only for high-school students. There are numerous art house films theaters, affordable restaurants, department stores, plus clothing and CD retailers. Make your date with friends at the **Hachiko dog statue**—a memorial erected for the faithful dog who came to meet his master at the station years after he had passed away—and from there, continue over to one of the world's most crowded intersections, familiarly known as **Scramble Crossroad** at Hachiko Square (featured in too many films to list here).

OTAKU TOKYO

A slightly younger and more anime, cosplay and rock music-oriented crowd would head to **Harajuku**, the next station up on the Yamanote train line from Shibuya. On weekends, street musicians and their audiences in wild costume and hairstyle can be found on the bridge between the Harajuku JR station to Yoyogi Park. Between Shibuya and Harajuku is the **Omotesando** area, where luxury shops from natives Issey Miyake and Hanae Mori, to foreign imports Chanel and Louis Vuitton, are centered.

The most recent hub for the true otaku nowadays is **Akihabara**, or Akiba for short. The area has for decades been known as the capital of consumer electronics, but the whole ward is now developing with the aid of Tokyo bureaucrats, into a major entertainment area. Many anime and game-related events take place here, and refreshments can be enjoyed in maid cafeterias, where young women dressed as, yes, maids, serve drinks and make conversation with usually young male customers. The area has become so popular, in fact, that there are now also guided tours for foreign tourists. The hit book, television drama and film *Densha otoko* a.k.a *Train Man* (2005) describes one typical type of "Akiba otaku"—an introverted admirer of pop idols who frequents Akihabara. Most of the filming for the movie was done

> **Cosplayer, Harajuku** photo: ©Andrew J. Stevens

on location here, and the saga is rumored to be based on real events and people. In either case, there are thousands of similarly clumsy and shy young men on the lookout for their own Hermes, the dream girl in *Train Man*.

A perfect cinematic Tokyo tour can be concluded in **Shinjuku**. **Kabukicho**, the area populated by yakuza-controlled bars, makes for a naturally perfect backdrop in many yakuza films, such as by ultimate horror auteur, Takashi Miike. Incidentally, you can sing a song or ten at **Karaoke-kan** (The Karaoke Palace) off the main thoroughfare of Kabukicho, if you want to pay homage to Scarlett Johansson and Bill Murray as drifters singing of heartache in *Lost in Translation* (2003). The area is also beautifully rendered in anime for Michael Arias's movie *Tekkon Kinkreet*.

Coincidentally, many of these independent art house features have premiered in the myriad theaters located between the Kabukicho area and neighboring Koreatown, **Okubo**. Kabukicho also has the famous **Golden Gai** Street, whose bars were filled with smoke and heated discussion of politics and art during the 1960s and 70s. Right in the middle of the scene were the career beginnings of new-wave directors like Nagisa Oshima, whose radical films borrowed from the real-life grit of the area.

Round up your Shinjuku stroll with an early evening drink at the primary setting in *Lost in Translation*—the **Park Hyatt Hotel's New York Bar**. There are actually two Hyatt hotels in the area, so be sure to go to the newer one. A magnificent view over Tokyo's glittering lights will make you promise to return to this multifaceted metropolis, and to catch more films featuring its various places. §

Eija Margit Niskanen has her M.A. from the School of Theater Film and Television at UCLA. She has traveled from her native Finland all the way to Japan, and seen some 30 countries on the way.

^ *Lost In Translation,* 2003 photo: ©Focus Features/Everett Collection
‹ **Park Hyatt Hotel, New York Bar** photo: ©Ben Hambury
[next page] **Angkor Wat Temple Steps, Cambodia** photo: ©yang shuo

04

THE EVERY WAR, THE EVERY EDEN
THAILAND + CAMBODIA

JOSE LUSTRE JR.
Most memorable experience in film/travel: For $1.50, the cheapest room I ever found was in a back alley in Bangkok. Plywood walls and an outdoor shower topped off the amenities.

THAILAND

• Kanchanaburi

Bangkok •

• Angkor Wat

CAMBODIA

Phuket •
[Hat Patong
Hat Karon
Hat Kara]

All of a sudden we're in Vietnam, not Pennsylvania. We are no longer watching a Russian wedding, filling up on the raucous laughter and dancing of the ensuing party. The cold, industrialscape of western Pennsylvania becomes a muddy river cutting through the feral jungles of Vietnam. All of a sudden, Michael, played by Robert De Niro, is holding a gun to his head and about to pull the trigger.

The sudden change in scenery is jolting; we are disoriented as the characters themselves try to make sense of their new surroundings. One

hour into the Oscar-winning *Deer Hunter* (1978), Michael and two of his buddies are imprisoned by the Viet Cong and forced to play Russian roulette. Wads of cash are thrown onto the table. Three bullets are placed in the chamber of the revolver. For the Viet Cong, this act of psychological warfare is a betting man's game.

Michael does pull the trigger, but not before turning the gun on the lead captor. The others are caught off guard. A barrage of gunfire leaves all but Michael and his friends dead. They float down the river to freedom, and are rescued by an American helicopter.

But the scene was filmed in **Kanchanaburi**, Thailand—not Vietnam. **The River Kwai**—itself an important military landmark—is standing in for one of the many rivers in Vietnam. This very location was also the setting for the climactic scene of *Casualties of War* (1987), in which a kidnapped Vietnamese woman tries to cross the river to safety but is shot by an American soldier's M-60. She falls off the bridge into the riverbank. The violence of both *Casualties of War* and *Deer Hunter* signified a new direction in American films.

∧ *The Deer Hunter,* 1978. photo: ©Universal/Everett Collection
‹ **Kanchanaburi** photo: ©Kristian Sekulic

The Vietnam War changed cinema. As the controversy surrounding the war grew, and support for the military engagement waned with stateside Americans, filmmakers began redefining the genre of war movies. They sought to portray the grim truths of the conflict. There were fewer lionized characterizations, fewer representations of invulnerable heroes. Protagonists were—for really the first time in the genre—subjected to moral dilemmas whose physical and psychological toll was expressed with unflinching realism.

Though Thailand had already established itself as a destination for film shoots (*Around the World in 80 Days* (1956), *The Ugly American* (1963) and *The Man with the Golden Gun* (1974) were made here), the post-Vietnam movement raised the standard in accurate storytelling. Filmmakers wanted to get as close to the Mekong Delta as possible. They wanted to show the humidity and grit of Saigon, the untamed jungles surrounding the Demilitarized Zone. Thailand was the answer.

Thailand's topography is nearly identical to Vietnam's. And while Thailand avoided colonial rule—the only sovereignty in Southeast Asia to do so— European-inspired architecture penetrated its borders. This meant the country had the visual ingredients directors and producers needed to approximate war-torn regions of Vietnam and Cambodia without their war-torn economies in the foreground.

Thailand's capital city of **Bangkok**, a three and a half hour bus ride east from Kanchanaburi, has been filmed as Saigon (*Deer Hunter, Good Morning, Vietnam* (1987), *Heaven & Earth* (1993)) and Phnom Penh in *The Killing Fields* (1984). The combustible energy of the capital and the tightly squeezed buildings in some of its districts make Bangkok a convenient replica of other large southeast Asian cities. And yet other parts of Bangkok feature old-world architecture and wider boulevards. All streets are overrun with pedestrians, cars, motorcycles, taxis and gas-powered tricycles, locally known as tuk-tuks. It is this combination of colonial influence and native freneticism that has allowed Bangkok cinematic mutability.

The nexus of tourist activity in Bangkok is the famed **Khao San Road**. As it was portrayed in *The Beach* (1997), this small road caters to the drunken whims of backpackers. Drink at the pubs or grab a bite at cheap restaurants. Exchange dollars into baht and buy knock-off designer goods. Travel agencies have also set up shop here and many tours in Thailand can be

< **Bridge, River Kwai** photo: ©iNmOKhem

arranged at Khao San. Khao San literally means milled or uncooked rice. The road served an important function historically in the country's rice trade. Further exploration of Bangkok, away from Khao San, will lead to excellent street food, regional beer and friendly exchanges with hospitable locals.

A few blocks south of Khao San, near the **Chao Phraya River**, is the red-light district of **Patpong**. What had been an R&R spot for American troops serving in Vietnam gained popularity with civilian tourists and became a hotbed of live entertainment in the following decades. Parts of *Deer Hunter* were shot here. Many of the area's bars feature go-go dancers and several establishments still advertise women performing explicit sexual acts, but curious foreigners are lured into these bars-cum-brothels to find themselves stuck with an exorbitant bill.

In a lot of ways, Bangkok is the antithesis of the rest of Thailand. The heat is inescapable during the summer. Unlike the mountains up north, there are no hidden waterfalls or streams that cool Bangkok. The daily gridlock around the city, and the noise and smog that come with it, belies the natural beauty of the beaches in the south. Tuk-tuks weave through the traffic as their high-pitched wail ricochets off squat buildings and strip malls. (A ride in a tuk-tuk will inevitably lead to a detour to a tailor, with whom drivers have struck a symbiotic arrangement—every tourist they bring in earns them free gasoline.)

But it makes sense. Bangkok is necessarily busy, as it acts as the central hub from which all of the nation's industries flow. Thailand's well-organized tourist infrastructure is anchored here, and having these services headquartered in one area will inevitably create a little ruckus.

Chiang Mai is an ideal destination for travelers seeking refuge from the chaos of Bangkok. An international airport and direct train routes to Bangkok serve the city. Situated in the northern mountains of Thailand, Chiang Mai stands as the cultural capital of the country. Visitors have the opportunity to witness life before industrialization, before a railroad connected it to central Thailand, before the ancient trading outpost famous for its handicraft became the country's second largest city.

American and European stores have sprung up in Chiang Mai. It's a mixed blessing for the locals. While increased foreign presence in local commerce

> **Khao San Road, Bangkok** photo: ©SqueakyMarmot

has a way of attracting more tourists and further stimulating the economy, this presence has also inflated prices and created unwelcome competition with Chiang Mai's artisans. The night bazaar and smaller stores still offer high quality jewelry and woodwork.

Those who want an even deeper immersion into local culture can arrange treks and excursions from Chiang Mai. Visitors hop on the backs of pickup trucks and head off into the mountains to learn about and see firsthand the local tribes who've inhabited the area for generations. These multi-day trips involve hiking through jungles, hills and rivers. Some even offer elephant rides. Nights are spent in villages where meals are prepared by local hosts. Accommodations are spartan and standards of hygiene are relaxed. Running water may not be available. Conversations with villagers range from the government's encroachment onto ancestral lands, to the varying attitudes toward tourists, to the perennial conflict against missionaries.

Scenes from *American Gangster* (2007) were shot in Chiang Mai. In the film, drug lord Frank Lucas, played by Denzel Washington, smuggles heroin from Thailand back to the U.S. Set in the late 1960s, Lucas's final shipment

is stuffed in the emptied coffins of seven American Vietnam War soldiers. Filmmakers have recreated wars in Thailand's scenic diversity—the mountains of Chiang Mai, the rivers and jungles around Kanchanaburi and even the noisy sprawl of Bangkok. It is no surprise then that even the pristine beaches of the south have served as the backdrop in recreating some of Southeast Asia's most gruesome scenes.

After the Vietnam War leaked through Cambodia's border, U.S. President Richard Nixon bombed the countryside where North Vietnamese troops had established strongholds. The covert operation killed 100,000 Cambodians. Two years later, Pol Pot and the Khmer Rouge overthrew the fragile government. In its pursuit to restore an agrarian society, the Communist regime evacuated Phnom Penh and forced millions into labor. Many worked or starved to death. The Khmer Rouge massacred ethnic and minority

^ *American Gangster,* 2007. photo: ©Universal/Everett Collection
‹ **Chiang Mai Mountains** photo: ©Sander Kemp

groups. Intellectuals—who were identified by their glasses or ability to speak multiple languages—were seen as threats and were murdered. During the four-year reign of the Khmer Rouge, 20 percent of all Cambodians died.

The decimation of Cambodia is a stark contrast against a history that included one of Asia's great civilizations. The Khmer empire once stretched over present-day Thailand, Laos and Vietnam. In the 12th century, they built Angkor Wat, one of the world's most culturally significant sites. The complex of Hindu and Buddhist temples covers an astonishing 90 square miles. In Wong Kar-Wai's *In the Mood for Love* (2000), the final scene was filmed within one of these temples. Chow Mo-Wan, played by Hong Kong actor Tony Leung, confesses a secret into a crevice on a wall. Having unburdened himself of a passionate but unfulfilled love, Chow walks away quietly. His secret is sealed within the ancient temples of **Angkor Wat**. The shots are long, the camera's movements are slow and a haunting score by composer Mike Galasso creates a lasting poignancy. Curiously, Wong's arthouse masterpiece and director Simon West's film adaptation of a videogame—*Lara Croft: Tomb Raider* (2001)—were shot within miles of each other, both in Hong Kong *and* Cambodia. The latter staging its first Asian action scene at **Ta Prom Temple** in its original game and later film versions. What many visitors remember about Cambodia are both the ancient grandeur of the Khmer civilization and the more recent military atrocity that tore the country apart.

The Killing Fields (1984) shows how the cruelty of Pol Pot and the influence of the Khmer Rouge ravaged Cambodia. The film was shot in Thailand and the American Embassy—whose occupants were forced to flee—was filmed in the southern island of **Phuket**. That building, which in real life is the Government House in Phuket Town, isn't far from what many consider the gateway to a tropical eden.

^ *Lara Croft: Tomb Raider,* 2001. photo: ©Paramount/Everett Collection
> **Ta Prom Temple, Cambodia** photo: ©photomorphic

Phuket is Thailand's biggest island and is on the western coast. It is connected to the mainland by a bridge and also has an international airport. A steady stream of tourists looking for the idyllic beach has helped bolster Phuket's economy; it is now one of the wealthiest provinces in all of Thailand. Even after the December 26, 2004 tsunami devastated the area, the resilience of both its people and economy helped rebuild the tourist infrastructure. It took less than a year for the island to bounce back.

Phuket is roughly the size of Singapore and offers a variety of beaches and towns to suit the varied tastes of visitors. **Hat Patong** is a lively, if not

seedy, area. **Hat Karon** and **Hat Kata** have soft sand and offer a more balanced nightlife. The northwestern shore of Phuket was once heralded as having the most unspoiled beaches on the entire island. Upscale spas and resorts have begun to plant themselves in what had been beautiful stretches of undeveloped paradise. Those seeking more secluded experiences do have the option of exploring some of Phuket's 39 surrounding islands. These islands might be backpacker haunts with rough accommodations, but they may just as likely be overdeveloped tourist magnets.

The variety of options in Phuket and its neighboring islands have attracted a plethora of filmmakers. In addition to *The Killing Fields, Casualties of War* and *Good Morning, Vietnam* (1987) were also filmed here. As filmmakers sought to portray the harshness of war in stark detail, the actual locations in Vietnam and Cambodia presented political and logistical impasses. So it was Thailand that offered itself as the canvas for these stories and proved that paradise is still paradise, even when staging a war. §

Jose Lustre Jr. saw *Apocalypse Now* as a 14 year-old and immediately planned a visit to Saigon. He made good on his promise and has since outrun a rock avalanche in the Himalayas, been hit by a truck in Indonesia and people-watched in downtown Ramallah. He recovers in Los Angeles, where he is a writer and an IT manager. He holds a degree in Print Journalism and Film Production from the University of Southern California.

05

GREAT SOUTHERN FILMSCAPES
AUSTRALIA + NEW ZEALAND

GEMMA BLACKWOOD
Most memorable experience in film/travel: First discovering the utter eeriness of Hollywood's Mulholland Drive by car at midnight.

Katherine Gorge
Kakdu National Park
AUSTRALIA
Watarrka National Park
Flinders Ranges
Blue Mountains
Sydney
Melbourne
Otara, Auckland
Whangara
NEW ZEALAND
Hobart
Ross
Port Arthur
TASMANIA
Queenstown
Dunedin

Australia. The great Southern continent

of high-contrast azure skies, even bluer coastlines, and a long expanse of dry red dust—in other words, the perfect landscape for the cinematographer's lens. It's been well publicized that Baz Luhrmann's latest epic film, *Australia* (2008), was deliberately scheduled for release alongside a massive international campaign for "Tourism Australia" and its film travel initiative. Yet Australia has already been represented on film in a multitude of ways. Many film locations move beyond the usual clichés and paint very different portraits of this country: not only the empty outback and its dangers but also the urbane and multicultural streets of the main cities, the wooded highlands and the snowy mountain regions. To see all of the iconic cinematic spaces that Aussie has to offer in a few days is a difficult task, because of the country's sheer size and the distance between major cities. On this armchair tour of the continent, first we'll head to the southernmost urban capital.

MELBOURNE

The second-largest city in Australia, **Melbourne** has featured in its fair share of films, often in disguise as disparate global cityscapes. More recently, a competitive exchange rate has seen it function as a substitute locale in

Hollywood films such as the Nicolas Cage vehicle *Ghost Rider* (2007), in which the inner city was improbably transformed into a Texan town. Another is the Anne Rice vampire chronicle *Queen of the Damned* (2002), pop singer Aaliyah's last feature film appearance before her tragic death in a plane accident. In this film, the laneway **Duckboard Place**, with its nineteenth century architecture in the inner CBD (Central Business District), became a makeshift English

∧ *Ghost Rider,* 2007. photo: ©Columbia Pictures/Everett Collection
‹ **Melbourne Skyline** photo: ©Neale Cousland

alleyway, and legend has it many Melbourne goths were called in as extras for some of the scenes. One that much older Hollywood film that was set in Melbourne was the classic post-apocalyptic *On The Beach* (1959), starring Ava Gardner and Gregory Peck. Shot in the bayside suburb of **Frankston**, literally on the beach, it was during shooting for this film that Gardner was reported to have quipped, "Melbourne sure is the right place to film (a movie about the end of the world)." Locals were infuriated for decades.

The popular Bollywood film *Salaam Namaste* (2005)—about a young couple of Indian expats working in Melbourne—also made the most of its inner city Melbourne setting, staging elaborate musical numbers at **Bourke Street Mall, Federation Square, St. Kilda** and the **Yarra River**. Another less likely film location hotspot is the **University of Melbourne**, located just north of the CBD. The car park underneath South Lawn is an amazingly designed gothic vaulted cavern; exciting enough for architecture aficionados, but the film connection can be made to *Mad Max* (1979) as the police headquarters. The University is a frequent film and TV backdrop, perhaps best featured in the locally and independently made *Love and Other Catastrophes* (1996), a colourful college-life comedy of the mid-1990s, starring prominent Australian actresses Frances O'Connor and Radha Mitchell. A grittier and decidedly darker representation of Melbourne launched the career of Russell Crowe—Geoffrey Wright's *Romper Stomper* (1992). The film about anarchistic and racist skinheads was largely shot in the immigrant suburb **Footscray**—those who've seen the film will instantly recognize the train station there.

While it's not cinema, a beloved soap opera considered to be "thoroughly Melbourne" and as comfortable as an old, faded pair of jeans is the long-running show *Neighbours* (1985 to present). Though the show never received much acclaim in the U.S., it *has* starred a number of Australian actors who have since gone on to establish successful Hollywood or pop music careers—Guy Pearce, Natalie Imbruglia and Kylie Minogue to name a few. Set in an average suburban *cul-de-sac*, the real life street **Pin Oak Court** in the Eastern suburb of **Vermont South** (used for exteriors only) has become a pilgrimage site for long-term fans, and it is easily the most visited film location in Melbourne by overseas visitors. This is primarily due to the hordes of British backpackers (the show has always rated highly in the U.K.) who visit the street by the busload when filming isn't taking

⟨ [top] **Federation Square, Melbourne** photo: ©Dave Townshend
[bottom] **U. Melbourne Parking Lot (from *Mad Max*)** photo: ©Alan Levine

place. The Melbourne Museum in the city centre also features an old interior *Neighbours* set that visitors are invited to walk through.

A couple of hours drive from Melbourne via Geelong takes you to the **Great Ocean Road** and the surf coast. **Bells Beach**—a real-life surfing mecca—was one of the fictional settings for the film *Point Break* (1991). Who could forget Patrick Swayze's almost romantic final moment with nemesis Keanu Reeves before he disappears into the Australian surf forever? Well, Bells Beach lives up to its ripping reputation as surfing hotspot, but unfortunately for fans, the location shot in the film was nowhere near it. You're actually looking at Oregon! Nonetheless, Bell's Beach is worth a visit, as is the rest of the immediate coastline. The Great Ocean Road drives over spectacular cliffs and prehistoric rock formations carved out by the seas (also featured in the aforementioned *Salaam Namaste*).

SYDNEY
Sydney remains one of the most spectacular, instantly recognized and photographed cities in the world, with its deep harbor, beaches and buildings constructed naturally around organic features. A good early film to watch before you visit is *They're a Weird Mob* (1966), by British filmmakers Michael Powell and Emeric Pressburger. In the film, Australia is seen through the eyes of a newly arrived Italian immigrant, and so makes much of exterior locations. Tourist icons such as **Bondi Beach, Manly** and **Neutral Bay** feature memorably.

Fox Studios has sent a number of high-profile U.S. productions to Sydney as well. The simulated urban reality of *The Matrix* (1999) is in fact the Sydney skyline. The John Woo-directed *Mission: Impossible 2* (2000) makes the most of the cityscape and harbor highlights: **Sydney Harbour Bridge** and the unmistakable **Opera House**. For those into Thai martial arts films and *über*-star Tony Jaa—a giant throughout Southeast Asia—the vendetta film *Tom-Young-Goong* (2005) was produced extensively around the Chinatown region off **George Street** in the CBD.

A couple of major children's films have made the most of locations in and around Sydney. Disney's *Finding Nemo* (2003), which transforms Sydney (and the Great Barrier Reef of Northern Queensland) into a technicolor splendor, brings light to all the surreal and kaleidoscopic elements of the submarine reef. Outside of Sydney, the adorable piglet movies for

> **Sydney Harbour Bridge** photo: ©Tomas Pavelka

children, *Babe* (1995) and *Babe 2: Pig In The City* (1998), made the most of a New South Wales highlands farmstead in the town of **Robertson**.

THE OUTBACK

The Outback of Australia, which incorporates much of Queensland, South Australia, the Northern Territory and Western Australia, continues to haunt the country's popular imagination, perhaps because the majority of its population lives on the coastline. Many memorable cinematic moments have occurred in this vast expanse. And though the less populated interior is often depicted as menacing and harsh, it also features the most iconic and unique landscapes of the country.

South Australia is more specifically a popular location for outback films, as the city of Adelaide is a convenient local production center (and cheaper to operate out of). Philip Noyce's *Rabbit-Proof Fence* (2002) is one such film, a true story about two Aboriginal girls who are taken from their home in 1931, and decide to walk back home to their community. This movie was partly shot in the **Flinders Ranges**. At the mining settlement of **Coober Pedy**, well known for its

NEW ZEALAND

Land of the long white cloud? More like land of the long wide-angle film shot. New Zealand has managed to reinvent itself in the last decade as a must-see place on the global set-jetting map, largely due to the success of one almost too-famous Hollywood blockbuster trilogy, Peter Jackson's *The Lord of the Rings* (2001-2003). Like smaller nations such as the U.K., the size of New Zealand makes it perfect for road trips and short stays, and the South Island is a great place to start your film sight-seeing tour. Flights can take you quickly in close to lakeside **Queenstown**, a cosmopolitan party town overflowing with both backpacker hostels and luxury accommodations. While you can no longer cohabitate (or co-Hobbitate?) with the stars in Queenstown, the film spots have maintained their aura, and a number of operators continue to offer 4WD road trips and flights of "everything Rings."

Once you've finished in Queenstown, fans of Jackson might also want to check out some locations from his earlier films. After a stop in University city **Dunedin**—used as backdrop for the Gwyneth Paltrow movie *Sylvia* (2004)—you will reach the old-English-seeming **Christchurch** (in the Canterbury region). Here, **Hagley Park** featured in Jackson's dreamy-psychotic film *Heavenly Creatures* (1994)—Kate Winslet's career starter

^ *Lord of the Rings: The Two Towers,* 2002. photo: ©New Line/Everett Collection

< **Queenstown, New Zealand** photo: ©cdarzases

about two matricidal young schoolgirls in the 1950s, and based on a real-life story. Hagley Park is a luscious pocket of botanical green and just a ten-minute walk from the city center. Then, a short drive from town, the tree-free hamlet of **Port Levy** on Banks Peninsula is another memorable site in which the girls are shown jetty-jumping and fantasizing.

As for the rest of the North Island, **Mount Taranaki** substituted for Mount Fuji in the medieval Japanese Tom Cruise vehicle *The Last Samurai* (2003). A range of beaches has made itself known on international screens. The Maori-named **Te Whanganui-A-Hei**, or **Cathedral Cove**, is a popular and pretty beach that featured in the latest installment of the Chronicles of Narnia *Prince Caspian* (2008).

The tiny town of **Whangara**—close to Gisborne—was the main setting for *Whale Rider* (2003), the spiritual coming-of-age film about a young teenage girl. Then, of course, there was *The Piano* (1993)— Jane Campion's Oscar winner shot on the spectacular **Karekare Beach** close to Auckland. If you are tiring from all these beaches, the downcast Auckland suburb of **Otara**—in particular, the public housing district on O'Connor Street— made the setting for the gritty film about contemporary Maori life, *Once Were Warriors* (1994).

Finally, to return to the work of our hirsute. Director Peter Jackson's first film *Bad Taste* (1987), was filmed at **Pukerua Bay**—his home town and the place where he honed his art. Considering this humble origin, his current popularity is not bad for a man whose films frequently contained more blood, pus and gore than your average Hollywood plastic-surgery clinic.

subterranean "cave" houses, an alien and forbidding landscape, the **Moon Plains** and the **Breakaway Mountains**, became the perfect setting for *Mad Max Beyond Thunderdome* (1985). The area was also used to film the camp Australian transvestite road trip movie *The Adventures of Priscilla, Queen of the Desert* (1994). *Priscilla* has made an indelible stamp on Australian life and culture, more recently being translated into a successful musical: a more iconic moment in the film occurs at King's Canyon at **Watarrka National Park** (close to Alice Springs), where one of the trannies (Terence Stamp) wants to climb the Canyon entirely in drag.

^ *Mad Max: Beyond Thunderdome,* 1985. photo: ©Warner Bros./Everett Collection
> **Watarrka National Park** photo: ©Neale Cousland

ABORIGINAL ORIGINALS

Hours north of Alice Springs, **Katherine Gorge** (or *Nitmiluk*, as the local indigenous population calls it) was a setting for the 1955 film *Jedda*. The water in the gorge is fresh and cold—and there's no need to worry about those frightening giant saltwater crocodiles, as featured in the horror film by Greg Lean Rogue (2007). It *does* have freshwater crocodiles or "freshies," but they're a much smaller type and generally afraid of humans! One of the first films to sympathetically portray the story of indigenous Australians, *Jedda* focuses on an Aboriginal woman (called Jedda) raised by a white family, only to be drawn back from her homestead into the natural world and her people. Falling in love with an Aboriginal man, Jedda is judged by the woman's original family for being too contaminated by the white Australians, and she and her lover are hence sentenced to death. Running from this fate, the two end up falling off a giant rock—now called **Jedda Rock**—to their certain deaths. While the Katherine Gorge Jedda Rock was filmed for the movie, the final dramatic scene needed to be reshot, as the negatives for this section were actually lost in a plane accident—the scene in the film we see today was actually re-shot close to Sydney at **Kanangra Falls** in the **Blue Mountains**.

A more recent film about Aboriginal life is Rolf de Heer's acclaimed *Ten Canoes* (2006), which is set in a time before English colonization and therefore the first feature film to make exclusive use of an Australian indigenous language. It is set and filmed in the **Arafura Swamp** region of **Arnhem Land** at the very north of Australia, one of the most remote areas of the continent, and only accessible to visitors who are granted permission from the local indigenous community. Locals also feature in the film, so on a cultural tour of the area, you might be lucky enough to meet a cast member.

DUNDEE COUNTRY

Close to Arnhem Land, there is **Kakadu National Park**, perhaps the most well-known world heritage area in Australia. Kakadu is generically known as "Dundee country" because of *Crocodile Dundee* (1986). It is perhaps still the most well-known Australian film for international visitors, if a

^ *Crocodile Dundee,* 1988. photo: ©Paramount/Everett Collection

‹ **Kakadu National Park** photo: ©Ashley Whitworth

little outdated twenty years on. Affable Aussie "bloke" Paul Hogan plays Mick Dundee. Hogan is the same actor who was responsible for the U.S. tourist campaign that continues to this day to make Aussies cringe: "throw another shrimp on the barbie" (for the record, Aussies say "prawn," not "shrimp"). *Crocodile Dundee* is thought to have been a significant factor in the massive rise in international tourism to Australia in the 1980s, not to mention the characterization of an entire people as friendly and open. A number of spots in Kakadu offer crocodile and wildlife-spotting excursions, which of course were also reinvigorated after the success of Steve "the Crocodile Hunter" Irwin's television programs. Irwin, who in his life promoted Australian wildlife, did more for the reputation of the croc than Lacoste.

TASMANIA

Interestingly, the beautiful island wilderness of **Tasmania**—the southernmost state of Australia—has yet to receive its definitive mainstream film representation. Indeed, it is probably still best known cinematically as the home of the Tasmanian Devil (Taz for short) of *Looney Tunes* animated fame! But there is yet another cartoon connection here, for fans of Japanese anime might be interested in STUIO GHIBLI's *Kiki's Delivery Service* (1989). Kiki's Tasmanian connection? The old baker's building in the small colonial town of **Ross** inspired the bakery central to the film's setting (the director, Hayao Miyazaki, was a big fan of Tassie).

One non-animated Tassie film of note is Richard Flanagan's *The Sound of One Hand Clapping* (1998), an underrated local film that prominently features many **Hobart City** icons, particularly the dock area around the Derwent harbor and the suburb of Glenorchy. Finally, an old Hollywood silent film, *For the Term of His Natural Life* (1927), about the harsh and tragic life of convicts in Tasmanian prisons and labour camps, was actually partly filmed in Tasmania, particularly around **Eagle Hawk Neck** and the convict town **Port Arthur**.

As one last tip for the incurable movie junkie in Australia, visiting film buffs would also be attracted to the **Australian Centre for the Moving Image** (ACMI for short), which is housed in the postmodernist arts and culture complex, Federation Square, in the centre of Melbourne. Similar in function

to the British Film Institute in London, ACMI has two cinemas, a video-game lab, an exhibition space and an interactive digital studio. Every July ACMI is one of the main hubs for the Melbourne International Film Festival (MIFF). Since it opened at Fed Square in 2002, the facility has featured a number of touring exhibitions focusing on directors such as Stanley Kubrick and Abbas Kiarostami, as well as innovative new media exhibits focusing on new turns in video art, computer games and Australian television. There's a low-key restaurant and bar located near the ticket counter that doubles as popcorn kiosk between session times. The planned new development for 2009—a new (and free) permanent display of film history for the public—promises even more delights and points of interest. ACMI is the kind of place where you're likely to catch the serious *cinephiles:* you know, that special brand of person who always stays until the end of the rolling credits ... oh yeah, and reads guide books about film travel. You just might be familiar with the type. §

Gemma Blackwood had an unhealthy youth of obsessive movie-watching, and armchair travel convinced her that the grass is always greener on the other side of the screen, which explains why she is currently finishing a research PhD, focusing on film and touristic desire at The University of Melbourne.

06

BEYOND THE AXIS OF EVIL

IRAN

MIKAEL AWAKE
Most memorable experience in film/travel: I've been to
Ethiopia several times, because many of my family members
live there. But when I went there a few years ago to shoot a
documentary at the Addis Ababa Fistula Hospital, I saw a side
of the country—the pain, the beauty, the quiet dignity—that
were revelations to me.

When President George W. Bush delivered his fateful State of the Union address in early 2002, fingering the Islamic Republic of Iran as one of three nations in the "Axis of Evil," a tense new chapter began between the two nations. The global political drama between Iran and the U.S. has since found its way into movie theaters, following the release of the American blockbuster *300* in 2006. In highly stylized action sequences, the movie recounts the mythic story of the Battle of Thermopylae (480 BC)—between an outnumbered team of Spartan warriors and the massive Persian army. Many, including Iranian president Mahmoud Ahmadinejad, argued that the film cast the ancestors of present-day Iran in a deleterious light. Ahmadinejad said of the filmmakers of *300*, "Today they are trying to tamper with history by making a film and by making Iran's image look savage."

The controversy underlies a relationship between Iran and much of the West that has in recent years grown increasingly tense. But if you are a cinephile willing to lay old stereotypes to rest and venture past the distracting curtain of international warnings, waiting for you within the borders of this alluring nation is one of the world's oldest, richest and most important cinematic histories.

A BRIEF HISTORY

Aside from its vast reserves of fossil fuels (ranked second globally, in both natural gas and oil), Iran has a well of cinematic history deep and rich enough to rival any other tradition. In 1905, the first movie house opened in Tehran.

In 1929, Ebrahim Moradi founded the ill-fated **Jahan Nama Studio**, the first and last film studio established in a provincial town. Though Moradi goofed on picking the best place to start a budding film enterprise in terms of commerce, he couldn't have chosen a more picturesque location for later visitors: the small port town of **Bandar-e Anzali** lies on the Caspian Sea, 170 miles northwest of Tehran. You won't discover any canisters of old silent

⟨ Shiekh Lotfollah Mosque, Isfahan photo: ©Serdar Yagci

films lying around town these days, but if you find yourself hankering for fish eggs, Bandar-e Anzali does happen to be the capital of Iran's thriving caviar industry, and the local caviar processing plant offers tours.

In 1932, five years after Al Jolson's *The Jazz Singer* broke the sound barrier in America, *Dokhtare Lor (The Lor Girl)* became the first Iranian film to follow suit. Though the industry often suffered under censorship and a lack of resources, the years before the Iranian Revolution were a boom time for Iranian film. The late 60s and early 70s ushered in an especially creative period known as the Iranian New Wave, but with the Revolution of 1979, film production in the newly dubbed Islamic Republic of Iran came to a grinding halt. It wasn't until the early 1980s that the new Shia Muslim government gave a group of talented young filmmakers the authority, support and encouragement to start working again, although with much stricter censorship guidelines. Depictions of suicide, homosexuality and nude women would be forbidden in Iranian cinema, as they continue to be today.

TEHRAN AT 24 FRAMES PER SECOND

Tehran is a bustling metropolis of nearly 20 million people, and every street corner seems to brim with history. Is this the same sloping hill that Ali raced down to win his shoes in the uplifting *Children of Heaven* (1997)? Is this the same textile factory in *Under the Skin of the City* (2001) where Tuba slaved? With a city this big you won't be able to see it all, but there are a few landmarks every traveler on a movie pilgrimage should try to hit.

The **Gheisar Bathhouse**, located in the southern part of Tehran near the bazaar, has a crumbling charm, with immense vaulted ceilings and cracked tiles, a kind of holy sanctuary for half-naked old men. Long before Viggo Mortensen was scrambling for his life in a bath house in *Eastern Promises*, Behrouz Vosoughi, who plays the eponymous lead role in Masoud Kimiai's tragic and bloody *Gheisar* (1969), murders one of the men responsible for raping his sister and killing his brother. The movie was an instant, angry classic and catapulted Vosoughi (and the bathhouse) into a local star.

Despite its inelegant name, the Institute for the **Intellectual Development of Children and Young Adults** (IIDCYA), more colloquially called **Kanoon**, is the sole organization responsible for producing the most significant films in the modern Iranian canon. Since 1961, this government-funded group has bankrolled such films as *Where Is the Friend's Home?* (1987), *Children of Heaven* (1997) and *Bashu the Little Stranger* (1989). It's a huge government organization, with 519 libraries and cultural centers, and its Cinematic Affairs department is one of their biggest and most prestigious divisions.

Held every February in Tehran, the 11-day long **Fajr International Film Festival** curates a wide array of foreign and domestic films, many of which often go on to compete (and on several occasions win) in the better-known European festivals like those in Cannes and Berlin. The 2008 Fajr Festival began with a star-studded red-carpet opening at the **National Grand Hall in Tehran**. But if you can't get tickets to the big premieres at the National Grand Hall, notorious for long lines of other impatient cineastes, don't lose heart. There are sure to be plenty of great viewing options at the **Cinematheque Hall of the Tehran Museum of Contemporary Art**.

RIDING THE NEW WAVE

Forugh Farrokhzad's 1963 short documentary film, *The House Is Black*, is a haunting meditation on life in an Iranian leper colony that marks a turning point in the national cinema away from schlock and melodrama, toward a more avant-garde realism. In twenty haunting minutes, Farrokhzad, whose career was tragically cut short in an automobile accident in Tehran only three years after the film's release, was able to captivate the sympathy of her countrymen. The widespread success of the film threw the problem of leprosy into the national spotlight, and the real-life leper colony where the film takes place, situated in the city of **Tabriz**, received substantial financial support from the government as a result of the film.

No discussion of the Iranian New Wave would be complete without mentioning Daryush Mehrjui's 1969 classic, *Gav (The Cow)*. The story, a mixture of absurd humor and crushing sadness, follows a poor farmer who has an unhealthy paternal love for his cow. When he finds his cow murdered, the farmer, played by Ezzatolah Entezami, suffers a severe nervous breakdown in which he becomes—in his own mind—a cow. The film was shot in a small village that this lone traveler had some difficulty locating, but allow me to make a brief, random suggestion while we're on the topic of slaughtered cows: if you're in Shiraz, grab a bite at the **Hamburger Stand Restaurant**.

> **Independent Cinema House, Tehran** photo: ©Frank Van Den Bergh

PILGRIMAGE TO KOKER

The name Abbas Kiarostami looms largely over contemporary Iranian cinema. As one of the most prolific and influential filmmakers in his country, and one of the most acclaimed directors on the international scene, Kiarostami's work over the past four decades is unrivaled for its poetic, no-nonsense depiction of life in modern Iran. He is noted for his use of nonprofessional actors, minimal dialogue and documentary-style shooting.

To film his groundbreaking *Where Is the Friend's Home?*, a parable about a young boy who must race to a neighboring village to return his friend's notebook and save him from being expelled, Kiarostami took his crew to

the remote village of **Koker**. Unbeknownst to Kiarostami at the time, this dusty, craggy village 200 miles northeast of Iran, would be the site of his later films *And Life Goes On* (1992) and *Through the Olive Trees* (1994). And according to the director himself (though disputed by critics), his Palme d'Or-winning classic, *Taste of Cherry* (1997), was a spiritual member of this Koker-trilogy, though set in Tehran.

A national catastrophe brought Kiarostami back to Koker after the release of *Where Is the Friend's Home?* In June of 1990, a massive earthquake that clocked in at 7.4 on the Richter scale struck on the rim of the Caspian Sea, northwest of Iran. It was the most devastating natural disaster in the country's history, killing 35,000 people and leaving hundreds of thousands homeless. Koker was deeply affected by the earthquake, and Kiarostami returned afterwards to chronicle the lives of the actual Koker denizens featured in *Where Is the Friend's Home?*

As one can gather from watching the documentary-style *And Life Goes On* (1992), which mostly follows a fictional director from Tehran to the earthquake's epicenter, the village of Koker is readily accessible by car. Traveling by car would be only fitting for a pilgrimage in honor of

^ *Where Is the Friend's Home?*, 1987. photo: ©Facets Video/Everett Collection
< **Masouleh** photo: ©Shahram Sharif

Kiarostami's work, which so often focuses on people in their automobiles. It's a long route, though not as circuitous as the one depicted in *And Life Goes On*, and rest assured that the roads are in better shape now than they were during filming.

HARSH REALITIES

At the time of this writing, the U.S. State Department had a Travel Warning listed for Iran. This means that the American government doesn't want its citizens to venture into Iran, on cinematic pilgrimages or otherwise.

There are reports of denied visas and visas inexplicably deemed useless upon arrival at the airport. On top of which there is no official American embassy in Iran, meaning that if you find yourself in a bind, the one place you can go is the U.S. Interests section of the Swiss Embassy (Africa Avenue and West Farzan Street, no. 59, Tehran). But film buffs can be sure that once the doors to Iran open again, a rich cinematic history lies waiting to be explored.

As a recent example of the potential danger lurking behind Iran's seductive charms, take the behind-the-scenes story of Mohsen Makhmalbaf's *Kandahar* (2001). This lyrical Cannes Jury Prize-winning film portrays, with arresting cinematography, the plight of a Canadian-Afghani woman trying to save her sister from a Taliban-controlled region of Afghanistan. Though most of the movie is set in Afghanistan, it was actually shot in the village of **Niatak** on the Iran-Afghanistan border. To capture the rocky, arid majesty of the setting, Makhmalbaf spent nearly three months in Niatak, only to discover while shooting that the town was located on a dangerous drug-smuggling route. Makhmalbaf is reported to have worn a disguise every day to avoid confrontations with the smugglers.

TO BE CONTINUED...

One of the sad pitfalls of experiencing a country solely through the lens of global politics is overlooking the vast wealth of culture that lies within its

^ **Rural Iran** photo: ©Neeku
> **Soldiers, Kandahar** photo: ©Lizette Potgieter

borders. Because of historical and current events, and negative portrayals in Western media, many travelers have a skewed image of Iran. Luckily, a new generation of young filmmakers, like Marjane Satrapi (*Persepolis*, 2007),

give Western audiences a multifaceted portrait. *Persepolis* depicts life as an Iranian exile in France. Films such as hers, and Iranian-American director Rahman Bahrani's—whose gritty realism has won the acclaim of established auteurs like Kiarostami—are poised to dispel old stereotypes while adding their own new, dynamic voices to their country's rich cinematic legacy.

Oh, and don't forget the basics: the work week in Iran runs from Saturday to Thursday, and many government offices, as well as private companies, are closed on Thursdays. Nothing is open on Friday, as it's the day of rest. Also, keep in mind that places to chow down will be limited during the month of Ramadan, which usually falls in late summer or early fall. Be sure to check before you book your ticket. ATMs, credit cards and traveler's checks are no good. Hard currency (Iranian Rials) is the way to go. §

In addition to co-writing the script for an upcoming biopic about marathoner Abebe Bikila, Mikael Awake recently went to Ethiopia to help film the IDA award-winning documentary, *A Walk to Beautiful*, about women suffering from fistula. He is working on a screenplay about a travel agent who is afraid of flying.

07

AN AMERICAN IN MOROCCO

MOROCCO

JOSE LUSTRE JR.
Most memorable experience in film/travel: Even in July, the mosquitoes were more menacing than the heat of the Libyan Desert. For several nights, I slept—and feverishly sweated—in a rain jacket, pants and shoes.

• Casablanca

• Marrakech
Ait Benhaddou •
Ouarzazate •

Rick's Café Américain is a den of opportunists, military officers and displaced Europeans. Hookah smoke softens the atmosphere as Sam, the piano man, plays jazz standards the expats would've heard back in Paris. Rick Blaine joins Captain Renault outside. A plane flies overhead, carrying passengers from **Casablanca** to Lisbon and, eventually, to a place far from the Nazi warpath.

"And what in heaven's name brought you to Casablanca?"
Captain Renault asks Rick.
"My health. I came to Casablanca for the waters."
"The waters? What waters? We're in the desert!"
"I was misinformed," says Rick.

Michael Curtiz's classic *Casablanca* (1942), one of the most-loved films of all time, triggers noir notions of love amid peril. Ingrid Bergman and Humphrey Bogart made us believe that Casablanca is a place where beauty is soft and delicate, the way Bergman appeared throughout the movie. Perhaps the lights in Casablanca twinkle the way her eyes always did.

But it isn't true. Light and camera filters were used each time Bergman was filmed. Rick's Café Américain was built on a studio lot in Southern California and the Casablanca of today is an industrial port town that has seen better days. This city is gritty and hard. There are no waters in its desert. Casablanca is worth visiting, just not for the reasons Old Hollywood wanted us to believe.

Unlike other parts of Morocco, Casablanca's proximity to Spain and the Mediterranean has given it a distinctly European character. It feels more like southern Italy than it does the gateway to Africa. Young men wear faded blue jeans and tight shirts emblazoned with the name of their favorite

---

∧ *Casablanca*, 1942. photo: ©Everett Collection
‹ **Casablanca** photo: ©narvikk

soccer player. Women dress in designer clothing or the traditional hijab. People congregate inside air-conditioned cafes and restaurants as they watch motorcycles and scooters zip by. Casablanca is where the old world clashes with the new.

The **Hassan II Mosque** is one of the city's main sites, itself a fusion of ancient and modern. Completed in 1994, the second largest mosque in the world has heated floors, a sliding roof and electric doors. It is also the only mosque in Morocco that non-Muslims can visit. The minaret is the tallest in the world at 656 feet; 25,000 can worship at any one time inside the mosque and another 80,000 can be accommodated in the surrounding plaza. A tour of the mosque reveals the intricacy with which thousands of craftsmen shaped the enormous structure. The marble floors are immaculate. A portion of the mosque is also built over open water and a glass floor allows worshippers to kneel directly above the sea.

Because of its role as the financial and industrial capital of Morocco—and because it is so close to the Strait of Gibraltar—Casablanca is where the forces of Islam confront those of Europe. This has led to problems, particularly in the last decade; suicide bombings in 2003 and 2007 killed civilians and were reportedly linked to Al-Qaeda. It makes sense then that Casablanca be retired as the cinematic representation of this city and be replaced with *Syriana* (2005) and *Babel* (2006), films that were shot locally and which capture the current religious, cultural and political dilemmas of the region.

In recent years, *Black Hawk Down* (2001), *The Bourne Ultimatum* (2007) and *Charlie Wilson's War* (2007) were all shot in Morocco. But landmark films by Louis Lumière and Orson Welles began the trend decades ago and over the years, the country's sand dunes, oases, beaches, harbors and canyons have stood in for scenes taking place across the Middle East and even as far away as Tibet. In an average year, between 20 and 30 films—many French and Spanish—are made here. Recognizing the inherent appeal of their topographically diverse landscape, Moroccans have established film studios to further develop this market and to entice moviemakers from around the world.

Ouarzazate is an eight-hour drive south of Casablanca. The city borders the Saharan desert and is also home to one of the most famous and

> **Hassan II Mosque** photo: ©Girogio Fochesato

well-preserved kasbahs, or fortified towns, in the region. Director David Lean shot parts of *Lawrence of Arabia* (1962) here. In the film, Turks massacred the people of Tafas, a village just south of Damascus, Syria. As T.E. Lawrence and his Arab forces pursue the marauding Turks, he utters the film's most famous line, "Take no prisoners!" The ensuing battle was filmed at Ouarzazate with the Moroccan army standing in for the Turks.

In 1983, hotelier Mohamed Belghmi built **Atlas Studios** at Ouarzazate to create infrastructure around the burgeoning industry that films like *Lawrence of Arabia* helped create. Leveraging the area's natural resources, Belghmi created a 370-acre primary lot on which sets have been constructed to simulate scenes in ancient Egypt, Rome and Israel. He also added a backlot, which comprises another 1,235 acres. Atlas Studios hosted production for *Kundun* (1997) and Ridley Scott used these sets for *Gladiator* (2000) and *Kingdom of Heaven* (2005).

Not far from Atlas Studios is **Ait Benhaddou**. This kasbah—a collection of attached homes with shared granaries, baths, ovens and shops—is one of the best-preserved in the area and was named a UNESCO World Heritage Site in 1987. It draws thousands of visitors each year, and has also been used as the backdrop for *The Last Temptation of Christ* (1988) and *Alexander* (2004). The complex is made entirely out of mud and straw and its color changes with the light—it becomes ruddier as the sun sets. Every rainstorm erodes Ait Benhaddou, so measures have been taken to preserve the structural integrity of the site and to protect even the simple geometric embellishments on many of the walls. The multilevel structures once functioned as a complete village but its watchtowers now look over the Ouarzazate River into a modern town. Most of Ait Benhaddou's original inhabitants and their descendants have moved to this town, though there are still a few families that continue to live within the kasbah, earning a living from tips and by selling Berber rugs and local wares.

Ouarzazate and the Atlas Studios showcase a desolate and sparsely populated region of Morocco, a blank canvas for the imagination of moviemakers. A

⌃ *Lawrence of Arabia*, 1962. photo: ©Everett Collection
< Ait Benhaddou Kasbah, near Casablanca photo: ©Quintanilla

four-hour drive north, however, is a city that is the cultural figurehead of Morocco. If Ouarzazate had an opposite it would be **Marrakech**, a city that is anything but mutable. Marrakech is a daily collision of culture and colors. It's what happens when commerce, noise and movement go unregulated.

When I visited Marrakech, I went out one day just after dawn, as the muezzin's voice crackled from the loudspeakers of Koutoubia Mosque. The air did not yet pulse with the freneticism of hawkers and their prey. The acts of bartering and negotiation had not yet begun—there would be thousands of deals and cons over the course of just one day. The temperature was not yet oppressive, not yet the reason to duck into cafes for a cool drink.

Navigation in Marrakech, like many of Morocco's old cities, relies less on street names than it does on small landmarks. I walked past the barbershop, took a left at the bakery, made a right at the store that still sells film. An alley led to a slightly larger path that ended in a much larger one. The arteries and veins of the medina all converged at **Djema'a al-Fna**, the heart of Marrakech.

In Alfred Hitchcock's *The Man Who Knew Too Much* (1956), Djema'a al-Fna is the backdrop for the film's pivotal scene. A French spy, whose attempts

at camouflage include blackface makeup and a large gown, is being chased through the square and the adjacent souqs. He runs past potters and dyers. At the same time, a touring American family, played by Jimmy Stewart, Doris Day, and a young Christopher Olsen, is enthralled by the raucous spectacle of the square. The family is not yet aware of the danger, and certainly don't suspect that their vacation will soon end.

Hitchcock shows rows of barbers and seamstresses, musicians, acrobats, and storytellers. As the spy runs through alleys, his assailant outpaces him and stabs him in the back. He staggers into Stewart's arms, and before dying, reveals information that will lead to the kidnapping of the family's son and the uncovering of an international assassination plot.

This scene was placed in St. Moritz, Switzerland in Hitchcock's original 1934 version of the movie. But in using Morocco for the remake, Hitchcock tapped into the mystique, the exoticism and the undercurrent of danger for which the "dark continent," as it is referred to in the movie, is known. Djema'a al-Fna is one of the largest and most striking squares in all of Africa. For centuries, it has been a nexus for travelers and filmmakers alike. Along with *The Man Who Knew Too Much*, portions of *The Mummy* (1999) and *Hideous Kinky* (1998) were filmed here. During the day, the plaza is occupied by stalls that sell freshly squeezed juices, nuts and dried fruits. Small monkeys, leashed at the neck, are trained to beg tourists for change. Cobras rise up from small baskets to the mesmerizing sound and movement of a snake charmer's flute.

As midday approaches, much of the action retreats to the surrounding souqs, a seemingly endless maze of craftsmen, smiths and artisans. But as the afternoon temperature begins to cool, activity increases and the entire plaza becomes a massive restaurant. Families roll in large grills and tables. Children point to the mounds of rice, olives, tomatoes, poultry and meat at their stalls as they vie for passing customers. Each stall is walled in by benches and tables where diners are invited to sit. Customers point to the meat they'd like grilled on the spot, and Djema'a al-Fna is overtaken with the smell of spices and freshly grilled meat and vegetables. Music blares from nearby stores and from live folk musicians. Entertainers and carnival games flank the food stalls. Here, you can seek advice from a fortune-teller or bet on which young boy will win a round of boxing. You can buy used dental equipment and dentures or browse the faded photographs and postcards that a man sells from a suitcase.

The festivity subsides around midnight, as men enter cafés to smoke cigarettes and drink coffee, and tourists retrace their steps back through the small alleys of the medina or hail taxis to upscale hotels outside of the old city. This is when Marrakech cools off. In these precious few hours before dawn, before the muezzin makes his first call, the city prepares itself for the day ahead and for the heat and the beautiful chaos that's sure to come. §

Jose Lustre Jr. saw *Apocalypse Now* as a 14 year-old and immediately planned a visit to Saigon. He made good on his promise and has since outrun a rock avalanche in the Himalayas, been hit by a truck in Indonesia and people-watched in downtown Ramallah. He recovers in Los Angeles, where he is a writer and an IT manager. He holds a degree in Print Journalism and Film Production from the University of Southern California.

< **Vendor, Djema'a el Fna** photo: ©Mathias Klang
[next page] **Tunisian Chott** photo: ©AGITA

08

A LONG TIME AGO... FAR, FAR AWAY— IN FILM

TUNISIA

LEE MIDDLETON

Most memorable experience in film/travel: Though not a fan of the desert, I'd like to spend more time in northern Africa, where the war on terror has had the unexpected consequence of making a region already famed for its hospitality all the more so. Plus, I dig the cool breezes under a kaftan.

Tunis

Tamerza •   Degache •   • Sfax

Nefta •   • Tozeur

Chott el Jerid •

Matmata •   • Ajim

Medenine

Tataouine

Seas of burnt umber sand and salty lakes so dry that the sinners among us can cross their crystalline surfaces with ease ... oases of palms dotted with human dwellings that appear to grow organically from the substrate upon which they sit ... bazaars that were part of ancient trade routes between the Mediterranean and Africa, where twisting lanes lead to merchants hawking actual antiques. With its otherworldly natural landscapes and cultural intactness, it's no wonder that the north African country of Tunisia has become a favorite movie stand-in for other eras and even galaxies. It's only a shame that beautiful Tunisia never plays itself.

Firmly establishing Tunisia as fantasy destination nonpareil, George Lucas' 1977 *Star Wars (A New Hope)* made the most of the desert country's amazingly lit moonscapes and unique architecture. Off a dirt road in southwest Tunisia near the border with Algeria, the dry white salt flat of **Chott el Jerid** stretches out for some 3,000 square miles. A lake that dries up almost completely in the hot season, this "chott" is the Sahara's largest and was once part of the Mediterranean Sea. It was also the location of that key scene in *Star Wars* in which a callow, rock-kicking Luke Skywalker gazes out across the Owen homestead toward not one but two suns.

Not far from Chott el Jerid is another of Tunisia's great chotts: **Chott el Gharsa**. Another vast desert salt shelf, Chott el Gharsa's deserts are home to the abandoned sets of "Mos Espa": the spaceport in *The Phantom Menace* (1999) where young Anakin Skywalker (pre-Darth Vader) grew up a slave. Now essentially a ghost town in the desert, the Mos Espa sets still contain elements recognizable from the film, like the spare parts dealer's shop. A 4WD vehicle and guide are recommended for finding Mos Espa among Chott el Gharsa's many dunes.

˄ **George Lucas,** 2008. ©Warner Bros./Everett Collection
‹ **Tunisian Chott** photo: ©Vangelis

Located a few miles from the Mos Espa set is the valley where Anakin Skywalker won his freedom in *The Phantom Menace*'s pod race scenes. The valley, which is below **Ongh Djemel** (Camel's Neck), was also the location of the Almásy-Madox expedition base camp in Anthony Minghella's *The English Patient* (1996). In the WWII drama based on the book by Michael Ondaatje, Count Almásy (Ralph Fiennes) and fellow geographers are

mapping the Sahara, an activity which will prove disastrous for the Hungarian-born protagonist when the war breaks out. The **Sahara sand dunes** around Ongh Djemel, and the mountain oasis of **Tamerza** (part of the **Djebel en Negueb** range), were used for scenes filmed in and over the desert, including the film's opening scene in which Almásy's doomed plane glides over those gorgeously undulating folds of ochre.

Another memorable location from *The English Patient* is found not far from Ongh Djemel, near the old Bedu caravan post of **Tozeur**. A stone's throw from Algeria, Tozeur was an historically important stop on the Bedouin caravan route from the desert to the Mediterranean coast. Just a couple of miles from Tozeur is the entrance to the "cave of swimmers" that Almásy and his team stumble upon in one of the Count's few purely happy moments. The cave, located at the summit of a hill outside the small town of **Degache**, becomes somewhat more funereal at the film's end when a weeping Fiennes carries the shrouded body of his lover, Katharine (Kristin Scott Thomas), out of the cave.

East of Tozeur and on the edge of Chott el Jerid lies the **Sidi Bouhel** Canyon, renamed the "Star Wars Canyon" by Lucasfilm. Standing in as the film's "Juntland Wastes," Sidi Bouhel saw the capture of R2-D2 by the Jawas (remember those glinting eyes from the crevices in the surrounding rock face?). The canyon also served as the place where Luke Skywalker and Obi-Wan Kenobi met for the first time, the Jedi-in-hiding intervening in an attack by the sand-people on his future protégé.

Though Harrison Ford's Han Solo had no scenes in the "Star Wars Canyon," the actor did end up filming here in his capacity as Indiana Jones in *Raiders of the Lost Ark* (1981). Conceived of and co-written by George Lucas, no doubt the use of several Tunisian locations in *Raiders* can be attributed to the moviemaker's experience filming *Star Wars*. **Sidi Bouhel** was used toward the end of the film in the Ark of the Covenant ceremony in which the Nazis and creepy French archeologist, Belloq, open that which should not be opened. Also near Tozeur, the **Sedala Desert** was used in *Raiders* for the scenes of the German excavation of the lost city of Tanis. Covering some 70 acres and using 160 Arab extras, the crew suffered through temperatures of 130 degrees while filming those scenes.

About 18 miles from Tozeur and 10 miles from the Algerian border is the oasis town of **Nefta**. Regionally known as the spiritual home of Sufism (Islam's mystical branch), Nefta is a major pilgrimage site and home to more than 24 mosques and 100 marabouts (shrines to holy men). Nefta was also the location for two distinctly non-mystical but no less major scenes in *Raiders of the Lost Ark*. The first was the scene in which Indiana Jones attempts to stop the airplane that he thinks is carrying the Ark of the Covenant to Nazi Germany. In the famous fight that ensues, Indy and an enormous German mechanic duke it out around the whirring blade of a flying wing's propellers. The second major scene filmed in Nefta was the chase sequence in which Indy-on-horseback catches up to the truck carrying the Ark. Indy ends up being thrown in front of the truck, from whence he hangs on the grill, slips and then uses his famous whip to hang on as he is dragged underneath the truck.

Back in the galaxy far, far away, Luke Skywalker's home planet of Tatooine was inspired by the actual town of **Tataouine**, located 200 miles southeast of Nefta and Tozeur. Despite giving Luke's hometown its name, most of the scenes of Tatooine were shot in the hills and villages surrounding Tataouine rather than in the town itself. The region around Tataouine was also used for filming *The Phantom Menace*. South of Tataouine and up on a hilltop, the **Ksar Ouled Soltane** is one of the biggest ksars (a traditional collective granary vault) in the area. This particular ksar is extremely well preserved, and was the location for some of the slave-quarter scenes from *The Phantom Menace*. North of Tataouine in the village of Hadada is the

Hotel Ksar Hadada, which served as the rear of the slave quarters, where Anakin's mother hints about his virgin birth to Qui-Gon Jinn (Liam Neeson). While on the topic of virgin births and Tataouine, the classic Monty Python film, *Life of Brian* (1979), also used the landscape around this Tunisian town for its final crucifixion scene.

More than 150 miles from Chott el Jerid where the exteriors were filmed, the village of **Matmâta** provided the interiors for *Star Wars*' Owen homestead. Filmed at the **Sidi Driss Hotel**, some of the murals and set dressings still remain in the hotel's inner courtyards, and Aunt Beru's kitchen and the dining room in which Luke argues with Uncle Owen about the fate of the droids remain recognizable. The Matmâta scenes made use of the unique sunken homes dug from the area's soft sandstone (the Sidi Driss being an example of this "troglodyte" style). The history of the building style in this area remains unknown, but it is likely that the first underground homes were built by locals hiding from Egyptian colonists given permission by the Roman Empire to take their land. Some of the local Berber residents still live in these traditional underground troglodyte structures.

STAR WARS PILGRIMAGE

The many sites used for filming the *Star Wars* films *A New Hope* and *The Phantom Menace* have reached pilgrimage status for fans of the epic series. Additional scenes filmed in Tunisia include:

Ongh Djemel:

- The valley below Ongh Djemel was also used for the arrival of Darth Sideous' apprentice, Darth Maul.

- Ongh Djemel was also the location from which Darth Maul launched the probes to hunt for the Naboo Royal Starship.

Chott el Gharsa:

- "The Yardangs" are rare and bizarre-looking wind-abraded sandstone outcrops found in the desert, resembling shark fins skimming the water. The yardangs near Chott el Gharsa served as the backdrop for the famous Jedi duel between Qui-Gon and Darth Maul in *The Phantom Menace*. In the base of one yardang is a metal frame where the springboard that launched Ray Park into his somersault was housed.

- The yardangs here are also where scenes of Queen Amidala's ship landing on Tatooine were shot.

- Near the Yardangs is a cluster of props that are the remains of the building where Anakin parked his pod-racer.

- Also near the Yardang field but closer to the dunes is the location for a scene from *The Phantom Menace* in which Qui-Gon and Jar Jar Binks leave for the spaceport but are stopped by Captain Panaka and Queen Amidala (disguised as her handmaiden, Padmé).

‹ **Matmâta, Medenine** photo: ©Jean-Claude Gallard

- A few hundred yards to the east (left) of the Yardang field and Repro Hadada set, is the amazing spaceport of the Mos Espa set. Among the remains are the Mos Espa gates, the gallery where Padmé, Shmi, Jar Jar and Qui-Gon watched the pod-race, the market place, and Jira's Nook. The set's incredible attention to detail still lend it a feeling of reality that is eerie when walking through its empty shells, surrounded by nothing but desert. Real pipes disappear into the ground, and electronic panels on the sides of walls and doorframes add to the "spacey" feeling.

La Grande Dune
- Six miles west of Nefta is a group of large sand dunes, which include "La Grande Dune," which was the location of the "Dune Sea," where C-3PO and R2-D2 wander aimlessly after making landfall on Tatooine.

- The Krayt Dragon skeleton that C-3PO passes in the desert was abandoned by the production crew in 1976. Made of fiberglass, the bones are almost intact and pieces can still be found in the sands of La Grande Dune.

- La Grande Dune is also the location where C-3PO hailed a Jawa sandcrawler.

Owen Homestead/Chott el Jerid
- A mile or so from the craters where the Owen homestead stood is a little dune area that was used for the beginning scenes in *A New Hope*, where C-3PO and R2-D2 have a fight after crashing on Tatooine.

- The scene where the Empire's stormtroopers track the droids down shortly after the abovementioned scene ("Look sir, droids !") was also shot at this small dune.

About 35 miles southeast of Matmâta, yet another ksar-turned-slave-quarter location from *The Phantom Menace* can be found in the major southeastern town of **Medenine**. At **Avenue 7 Novembre**, a bustling bazaar houses the **Ksar Medenine**, which served as the location where young Anakin says goodbye to his mother before leaving with Qui-Gon. The narrow street in which the filial farewell occurs runs behind the bazaar square.

Heading north up the coast, the harbor town of **Ajim** on **Djerba Island** served as the sleazy spaceport "Mos Eisley" in *A New Hope*. The most important location in Ajim is **Chalmun's Cantina**, which used to be a traditional Berber bakery. It is in this bakery-turned-space cantina that fresh-off-the-boat Luke Skywalker and wise old Obi-Wan first meet swashbuckling Han Solo (and the world met a bar full of aliens). Also on Djerba Island and overlooking the **Gulf of Gabes** are two mosques that served respectively as the locations for Obi-Wan's home and the Anchorhead entrance to Mos Eisley. Once primarily a place for sponge fishermen, Djerba Island has become a popular tourist destination.

> **Djerba** photo: ©Ermin Gutenberger

Continuing north along the coast, one reaches **Sfax**, Tunisia's second largest city and stand-in for 1938 Cairo in *The English Patient*. The **medina** (the old walled part of every Arab town or city) at Sfax was the location for the scene where Katharine buys a bauble, only to bump into a stalking Count Almásy, who informs her that she's been ripped off. In 1938, Cairo's population counted fewer than two million. Its vastly increased populace and other physical changes meant that the city could no longer play itself, thus allowing smaller cities like Sfax to win the role. In fact, Sfax is not known as a tourist destination, and as a result its medina is supposedly a good place to acquire antiques for sale to a predominantly Tunisian crowd. Heading up the coast from Sfax toward Sousse, the port town of **Mahdia** was also used for additional Cairo city scenes as well as the invasion of the strategic port of Tobruk (northeastern Libya) in *The English Patient*.

Up the coast from Mahdia, the town of **Monastir** stood in as Jerusalem in Monty Python's *Life of Brian*. Most of the film was shot in the **Ribat**, Monastir's fortified Islamic monastery and once the setting for Franco Zeffirelli's TV production, "Jesus of Nazareth." The Ribat, with its maze of walls and passages, is open to the public. *Life of Brian* also used the **Kasbah at Sousse** to stand in for Jerusalem's city walls. The Kasbah is now a museum, and contains Tunisia's second most important collection of Roman mosaics (after Tunis' Bardo Museum collection).

For all its beauty, Tunisia rarely gets to play itself. Sousse's old city of **Kairouan** also played the role of Cairo, this time circa 1936 for *Raiders of the Lost Ark*, despite the fact that the town's traditional whitewashed houses with their blue details bear no resemblance to Cairo's architecture. And lest one get the impression that Tunisia is living in another age, the production crew of *Raiders* had to spend a whole day in Kairouan removing 350 TV antennas from houses around the building that served as **Sallah's home**, where the famous "bad date" scene plays out.

︿ *Raiders of the Lost Ark,* 1981. photo: ©Everett Collection
‹ **Sousse Medina** photo: ©Igor Grochev

Kairouan was also used in *Raiders* for other Cairo street scenes. The most famous is probably Marion's kidnapping and the ensuing chase in which Indy confronts an Arab who makes a show of his swordsmanship. In the script, Ford was meant to use his whip to beat the swordsman. However, with the entire crew down with dysentery at that point in the filming, Ford lacked the patience for the complicated scene and supposedly suggested to Spielberg that they just "shoot the fucker." Thus was born one of cinema's funniest fight-scene denouements. Kairouan also is the most important Muslim holy city after Mecca, Medina and Jerusalem.

A final stand-in for Cairo, Tunisia's capital at **Tunis** also served in Anthony Minghella's *The English Patient.* A former foreign minister's private residence in Tunis was used for two scenes set in the British Ambassador's Cairo residence: the dinner party at which a jilted Almásy shows up drunk and belligerent, and the Christmas celebration in which Almásy and Katharine make love while her husband, dressed as Santa, and the rest of the Pommies sing Christmas carols and God Save the Queen. §

Lee Middleton has traveled and worked in 34 countries across five continents. She currently resides in Africa.

09

BUILDING FANTASIES: EAST AFRICA IN FILM

EASTERN AFRICA

LEE MIDDLETON
Most memorable experience in film/travel: Traveling and working across east and central Africa, I've hiked with the gorillas, flown in bi-planes, tracked giraffes by moonlight, been rudely awakened by hippos, and avoided donkey poo in meandering Swahili lanes. Collectively my time in this region has proven that reality can surpass cinema, especially in Africa.

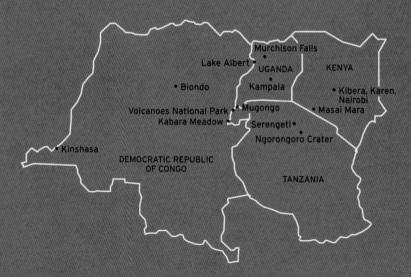

Murchison Falls
Lake Albert
UGANDA
KENYA
Biondo
Kampala
Kibera, Karen, Nairobi
Volcanoes National Park
Mugongo
Masai Mara
Kabara Meadow
Serengeti
Kinshasa
Ngorongoro Crater
DEMOCRATIC REPUBLIC OF CONGO
TANZANIA

Hollywood's fascination with Africa first

took hold in the 1950s. Initially focusing on the continent's eastern and central nations, the "African films" (i.e., films made in and about Africa, as opposed to *by* Africans) of the period gave Technicolor form to hitherto vague notions of the "the dark continent." Perhaps unsurprisingly, the bulk of these films enlisted East Africa's iconic natural landscapes as locations: the classic Kenyan and Tanzanian savannas with their thundering herds and acacia-tree horizons; Uganda's crystalline lakes, volcanic moonscapes and enormous flocks of colorful birds. This rather narrow view of the continent both fueled a billion-dollar safari industry and "branded" Africa-the-concept with a particular look, not to mention preconceived ideas related to the invincibility of nature, personal freedom, and the ongoing legacy of imperialism—all of which continue to replay both in African films and Western imaginations.

The European desire to explore and tame Africa has been at the heart of a number of classic American films. In *The African Queen* (1951)—one of Hollywood's most enduring accounts of this will to overcome—Rose Sayer (played by Katharine Hepburn, whose participation in the film was

contingent on it being shot on location), bluntly states, "Nature is what we were put on earth to rise above." This principle is put to the test in multiple trials that range from titillating to terrifying. One of the first indications that Rose is no shrinking violet comes when the film's eponymous steamboat hurtles over the rapids at **Kabalega Falls National Park**. Afterward, a flushed Hepburn exclaims to a confounded Humphrey Bogart, "I never dreamed that any mere physical experience could be so stimulating." Now a part of **Murchison Falls National Park** (per the British

^ *The African Queen,* 1957. photo: ©Everett Collection
< Murchison Falls National Park photo: ©Klaas Lingbeek van Kranen

name for the falls, which explode violently through a narrow cleft in the Rift Valley escarpment) in northwest Uganda, it's one of the country's largest and most visited preserves, thanks no doubt in part to the famous sequence.

Somewhat further down the river (and into the courtship of Rose and Bogart's Charlie Allnut), the *African Queen* bogs down in a papyrus quagmire, forcing Charlie to literally pull the boat through the muck, from which travail he emerges covered in leeches—a scene that remains burned in many a moviegoer's mind. The real horror is yet to come, when Hepburn and Bogart are both forced back into the leech-infested waters to continue on toward their target, the German warship *Louisa*, which is busy patrolling Uganda's **Lake Albert**—the northernmost of Africa's Great Lakes, and part of the complicated upper Nile system of lakes and rivers that include the Victoria Nile.

Stimulating physical experiences abounded behind the scenes of the "African films" too. Filmed entirely on location across East and Central Africa, the 1950 production of *King Solomon's Mines*—the first major Hollywood effort filmed on this scale in Africa—captured groundbreaking footage that MGM would employ repeatedly over the years, and the film won a Best Cinematography Oscar. But the acquisition of this prized celluloid also left stars and crew debilitated by malaria and dysentery, shooting in locations from Zaire's **Biondo** village (outside **Kisangani** town in the northern part of what is now the Democratic Republic of Congo) to what are now the safari capitals of the world: the great plains of Tanzania's **Serengeti** and Kenya's **Masai Mara**. Biondo was also used as a base for *The African Queen*'s cast and crew, who all got sick when dishes were washed in contaminated river water, as recounted in Hepburn's memoir on the making of the film. Only Bogart and director John Huston were immune, which they attributed to their steady diet of scotch. Bogart later said, "Whenever a fly bit Huston or me, it dropped dead."

The Masai Mara was more recently the location for a famous scene in Sydney Pollack's *Out of Africa* (1985), where Robert Redford as Denys Finch Hatton washes Karen Blixen's hair by the side of the **Mara River** whilst reciting Samuel Taylor Coleridge's *The Rime of the Ancient Mariner*. Legions of sensitive shampooers might be amused to discover that the seemingly swept-away Meryl Streep (playing Blixen, the poet laureate of romanticized Africa) actually spent the duration of the scene in a panic. A

‹ **Serengeti Plain** photo: ©Michel de Nijs

nearby pool, full of hippos—Africa's most dangerous animal—had the actor summoning the full force of her legendary skills to achieve that look of well-lathered bucolic bliss. (More on *Out of Africa*, perhaps the ultimate "African film," in a minute.)

The struggle between humans and wild animals naturally plays a great part in films about Africa. The classic *Hatari!* (1962) consists largely of languorous, beautifully shot takes of plains animals from giraffes to zebras to rhinos thundering across Tanzania's **Ngorongoro Crater** while John Wayne and his team of zoo-trade rustlers attempt to lasso them from open jeeps. In *Mogambo* (1953), Clark Gable played the zoo-employed safari hunter (seems Hollywood didn't want to present moviegoers with dead animals) who becomes entwined in a love triangle with Ava Gardner and Grace Kelly as they comb the wilds of the Masai Mara and Serengeti for potential prizes, heading ultimately for gorilla country.

Entering real gorilla country, *Gorillas in the Mist* (1988) upped the bar for Hollywood's wildlife cinematographers. Based in part on the book of the same name, the film depicts the career of Dian Fossey (played by Sigourney Weaver), the passionate champion of the charismatic primates. Fossey's uncompromising position on keeping people—tourists and poachers alike —off "her mountain" probably led to her still-unsolved murder at Rwanda's **Karisoke Research Center**, which figures prominently in the film. Thanks in part to Fossey's work bringing attention to the near-extinction of one of our closest genetic relations, the mountain gorilla's population increased from some 200 in the early 80s to a current count of about 700 in and around the forests of the Virunga Mountains. Rwanda's **Volcanoes National Park** (part of the Virungas) in the country's mountainous northwestern region served as the backdrop for much of the film. Today visitors can buy a permit to hike Volcanoes Park and spend an hour with the gorillas in the company of Rwandan trackers and guards—an experience every bit as awesome as the film would have you believe.

More intrepid primate-lovers might head to the Democratic Republic of Congo's side of the Virungas, where legendary wildlife biologist George Schaller ran his research from a small cabin in the **Kabara Meadow**—the same location from whence Fossey was expelled by Congolese military men in the film's beginning (and unfortunately still a region dominated by men

> **Volcanoes National Park** photo: ©Guenter Guni

with guns). Following her expulsion from the country, Fossey made her way to **Rosamund Carr's flower plantation at Mugongo** in Rwanda. Doyenne of the African expatriate community, Carr transformed her destroyed plantation into an orphanage after the country's 1994 genocide, renaming it "Imbabazi" ("a place where you will receive all the love and care a mother would give").

Africa's recent history, of course, has all too often been one of armed struggle. Another place of refuge during the Rwandan conflict was Kigali's **Hôtel des Milles Collines**. The 2004 film *Hotel Rwanda* depicts the now-

infamous genocide and the heroics of Milles Colline's manager, Paul Rusesabagina (played by Don Cheadle), whose efforts helped save more than a thousand people. Though the actual Milles Collines was not used in the film (the majority of which was shot in South Africa), the faithful reproduction of its poolside remains quite recognizable when visiting the real thing, which thankfully has returned to the business of sunbathing and beer.

Rwanda's neighbor, Uganda, suffered a different sort of terror from 1971-1979, during which time military dictator and president Idi Amin was responsible for the death of as many as 500,000 Ugandans in his bid to maintain absolute power. A fictionalized account of Amin's reign based on the book of the same name, *The Last King of Scotland* (2006), was largely filmed on location in **Kampala**, Uganda. The movie's final scene makes creative narrative use of the 1976 hostage crisis, in which Amin allowed a Palestinian-German hijacked Air France plane to land at **Entebbe Airport**. The scene was in fact filmed at Entebbe Airport, the country's main international hub, located on the shores of Lake Victoria about 20 miles from Kampala, Uganda's capital.

Speaking of despots we love to hate, take a gander at Mobutu Sese Seko, wearing his trademark leopard-skin hat in the 1996 documentary *When*

˄ *Hotel Rwanda,* 2004. photo: ©United Artists/Everett Collection
‹ Hotel des Milles Collines photo: ©Genvessel

We Were Kings, which recounts the legendary 1974 "Rumble in the Jungle" between Mohammed Ali and George Foreman. The fight, organized by a rising young promoter named Don King, took place in **Kinshasa**, Zaire (now the Democratic Republic of Congo) at **May 20 Stadium**. Pegged as the underdog but beloved by the Congolese, Ali rocked the world when he knocked Foreman out with a left hook in the eighth round to chanting cries of "Ali, bomaye!" (Ali, kill him!)

Killing of a different sort is the topic of 2005's *The Constant Gardener*, based on the John LeCarre novel, whose Big Pharma company "BBB" uses HIV-positive residents picking up free anti-retrovirals in Nairobi's **Kibera** as guinea pigs. The largest slum in sub-Saharan Africa, Kibera covers some 600 acres and is home to about 1 million people, most of whom live in makeshift huts with no plumbing or sewage. The theater troupe that stages a play about AIDS in the film's beginning is Nick Reding's SAFE group, which performs HIV/AIDS awareness street theater along truck routes from Mombassa to Nairobi.

Not far from the slums of Kibera is the leafy suburb of **Karen**, one of contemporary Nairobi's most expensive and desirable addresses. Locals will tell you that the area was named after Karen Blixen (better known as Isak Dinesen) because when villagers were headed that way, they would say they were "going to Karen." Blixen's original house was not used in the filming of the movie, but the recreation was so exact that approaching the driveway of the original will immediately set the theme music of what's arguably the ultimate instance of the "African film" ringing in your head.

Setting the parameters for Western fantasies of Africa since its release, *Out of Africa*, based on Blixen's book of the same name, romanticized and lamented the disappeared time and place the "African films" simultaneously introduced and ushered out, in such a way that people would forever chase its memory.

The scene in which leads Meryl Streep and Robert Redford fly over Kenya's **Lake Nakuru** and its masses of pink flamingos remains one of cinema's most memorable and beloved images ("They rise in a cloud, like dust from a beaten carpet; they are the color of pink alabaster," wrote Blixen of the sight). The fantastical vision evokes an exhilarating sense of ever-elusive freedom and romance that have become synonymous with popular Western ideas of Africa. Though Nakuru's flamingo population has decreased dramatically from 2 million to a sad 30,000 (blame industrial pollution and siltation from deforestation), the flamingos do still visit **Lake Nakurua National Park**, located just 160 kilometers north of Nairobi. Bring your own biplane and doomed romance.

Geographic verisimilitude, however, has its limits. Using one location as a stand-in for another is common practice in filmmaking, and certainly in Africa, it has often become a necessity due to constantly shifting political and logistical challenges. Another take on the flamingos-over-water image features in *The Constant Gardener*. This time, however, the avian glide over Kenya's **Lake Magadi** is more harbinger of death than symbol of freedom. Deep in the heart of southern Masai land, Magadi is a 104 sq kilometer soda lake (its supersaturated tones onscreen being a combination of the lake's pH and *City of God* director Fernando Meirelles's aesthetic propensities). Completely surrounded by vast salt flats, it is often the final destination for treks from the Nguruman escarpment or the Loita hills. But though filmed at Lake Magadi, the movie would have us believe that the lake upon whose shores Ralph Fiennes awaits his murder with fatalistic zeal was actually **Lake Turkana**, the world's largest alkaline lake. A hot and arid place of howling winds, volcanic rubble and Nile crocodiles, northern Kenya's Lake Turkana and its environs are also a World Heritage Site, forming one of the country's wildest national parks. And though in fact it wasn't among the Great Lakes discovered in the course of Sir Richard Burton and John Hanning Speke's 1857 expedition to find the source of the Nile—a quest that nearly killed both, several times over—in *Mountains of the Moon*, Bob Rafelson's 1990 film recounting the expedition, Lake Turkana was ironically used to portray Tanzania's **Lake Tanganyika**, the watery body that the adventurers did arrive at, hoping (in vain) that they had finally located the source of the mighty Nile. §

Lee Middleton has traveled and worked in 34 countries across five continents. She currently resides in Africa.

10

KEEPING IT REAL IN SOUTHERN AFRICAN FILM
SOUTHERN AFRICA

LEE MIDDLETON
Most memorable experience in film/travel: First flew at 11 months. She vomited across the Pacific to the horror of fellow first-class passengers. Having no recollection of the experience, she wishes it had been filmed.

Unlike the romance of East African films

and the otherworldliness of North African cinema, films set in Southern Africa seem to focus largely on conflict: from historical conflicts like the Anglo-Zulu War to the struggle against apartheid to the contemporary battle of people living with and dying from HIV/AIDS. The internationally recognized cinema of Southern Africa also includes many more films actually made by Africans than does the rest of mainstream "African film." As a result, a refreshingly broad variety of locations—it's not all gorgeous landscapes and wild animals—and African characters, both black and white, are represented in them.

In film as in history, South Africa (the country) has seen more than its share of conflict. One of Hollywood's earliest films depicting war in South Africa is *Zulu* (1964), depicts the Battle of Rorke's Drift in the **Drakensberg Mountains of KwaZulu Natal**. On January 22, 1879 the British army suffered its greatest colonial defeat ever at Isandlwana, where Zulu King Cetshwayo's roughly 25,000 warriors wiped out an entire British regiment. Later that same day, more than 4,000 Zulus attacked another 139 British soldiers at the nearby Rorke's Drift Mission. In what is considered one of the great military defenses of all time, the Brits held their garrison, suffering only 17 casualties and earning the regiment 11 Victoria Crosses. *Zulu*, which was Michael Caine's first leading role in a movie, was filmed in the Northern Drakensberg at the **Amphitheatre**, in what is now the **Royal Natal Park**. The Isandlwana scenes were also filmed here, near the **Mont aux Sources Hotel**. About 200 yards from the Amphitheatre is the location where the film's impressive opening scene of a Zulu mass wedding was shot.

South Africans today are fighting a different and perhaps even more destructive battle than did their predecessors. HIV/AIDS has decimated entire communities around the country and continent, with the South African province of KwaZulu-Natal being particularly hard hit. Contemporary filmmakers in South Africa have naturally been drawn to this crisis as a narrative subject, producing several of the country's most acclaimed films as a result. *Yesterday* (2004), the first ever feature-length

‹ KwaZulu Natal photo: ©Jeremy Richards

Zulu-language film, focuses on the life of its title character, a village woman from rural KwaZulu-Natal (played by Leleti Khumalo) who contracts HIV from her husband, a gold miner who works near Johannesburg. Filmed in **Okhombe village** near the town of **Bergville** in the aforementioned Drakensberg Mountains, the film plainly depicts the terrible physical and social difficulties of living with this disease in rural South Africa.

Another movie about the effects of HIV/AIDS on rural South African communities, directed by South African David Hickson and written and produced by American W. David McBrayer, is *Beat the Drum*. The 2003 film opens with shots of the beautiful **Ukhahlamba Valley**, also in the Drakensberg Mountains. But the reality of the film's tale quickly overwhelms the sweeping vistas: in a small village, young Musa has lost both of his parents to AIDS. *Beat the Drum* tells the story of Musa's quest to find his uncle in **Johannesburg**, who he hopes can help him earn enough money to buy his grandmother a cow. Set in rural KwaZulu-Natal and the mean streets of the South African capital, Musa's story is all too common: dodging muggers and thieves, he becomes part of a world of street kids, most of whom are also AIDS orphans.

Another contemporary South African film with roots in the HIV/AIDS crisis and its impact on urban poverty is Gavin Hood's *Tsotsi* (2005). Adapted from the book by Athol Fugard, South Africa's first Oscar-winning film follows David, a teenager who goes by the street name, Tsotsi. Having run

away from his HIV-stricken mother and abusive father, Tsotsi ("thug" or "gangster" in Soweto slang), makes his rounds in the streets of **Soweto**, Johannesburg. An area whose name is an abbreviation for "South Western Townships," Soweto came to the world's attention on June 16, 1976, when mass student protests against the apartheid government's policy requiring an Afrikaans-based education climaxed with police opening fire on 10,000 students. Five hundred sixty six people died, and the Soweto uprising, as

^ *Tsotsi,* 2006. photo: ©Miramax/Everett Collection
< **Soweto** photo: ©Steven Allan

it became known, sparked economic sanctions from without and further resistance within South Africa. *Tsotsi* was largely shot on location in this vast collection of townships, whose shacks and poverty make a compelling backdrop for the ruthless behavior exhibited by many of its characters.

Another film shot in Soweto is Spike Lee's 1992 biopic *Malcolm X*. Though Malcolm X never traveled to South Africa, the movie's end likens him to fellow rabble-rouser Nelson Mandela, who appears onscreen as a schoolteacher in a Soweto classroom (the scene was shot just two years out from his 27-year political imprisonment). Today Soweto remains one of the poorest and most populous of Johannesburg's townships, though its importance in history, politics, music and fashion make it a place of continuing cultural significance.

South African Jamie Uys' 1980 satire about the evils of civilization and city life, *The Gods Must Be Crazy*, takes place only 600 miles away from the madness of Johannesburg, yet seems other-worldly. Set in the **Kalahari Desert** of South Africa and Botswana, the film tells the story of Xi, a Sho (Bushman) from the Kalahari who leaves the bush on a quest to find the end of the world. Xi's mission is to rid his family of the mysterious "evil thing" that fell from the sky, disturbing their noble-savage existence—to wit, a Coca-Cola bottle. Xi's journey ends at the top of a cliff, beneath which a solid layer of clouds obscures whatever lies below. The film's "end of the world" is actually **God's Window**, in what was then the Eastern Transvaal, now **Mpumalanga Province**.

Mpumulanga is also home to the **Secunda Oil Refinery**, the second largest in South Africa, where gasoline and diesel fuel are produced from coal liquefaction. The refinery is the backdrop for the story of Patrick Chamusso (played by Derek Luke) as told in the 2006 film *Catch A Fire*. Wrongly accused of conspiring in an African National Congress plot to bomb the refinery, Chamusso becomes politicized by the injustices of his arrest and torture, and is later instrumental in a second, semisuccessful bombing. Written by Shawn Slovo, daughter of South African Communist Party leader Joe Slovo, and directed by Phillip Noyce, the film was shot at many of the actual locations involved, including the Secunda Oil Refinery itself, which was once a symbol of the apartheid government's self-sufficiency in the face of international economic boycott. The film also used other historic

> **Kalahari Desert** photo: ©Addictive Picasso

WELCOME

ROBBENEILAND

WE SERVE
WITH PRIDE

ONS DIEN MET TROTS

WELK

locations such as the **ANC villa** in **Maputo, Mozambique**, for scenes of Patrick's politicization and training. Other scenes meant to be in Maputo were filmed in the Johannesburg suburb, **Yeoville**.

From the '80s until the fall of apartheid, internationally produced films set in South Africa focused almost exclusively on the apartheid state and its heroes and villains. As a result, these films were never shot in the country. Richard Attenborough's *Cry Freedom* (1987), which tracks

the friendship between Black Consciousness Movement leader Steve Biko (Denzel Washington) and *Daily Dispatch* newspaper editor Donald Woods (Kevin Kline), was filmed almost entirely in then-stable neighbor Zimbabwe. The film's dramatic opening sequence, in which the South African police raid Cape Town's Crossroads Settlement, was filmed in **Mbare**, near Zimbabwe's capital, **Harare**. Mbare was also used for the tour that Biko takes Woods on to educate the white liberal about life in an African township.

In contrast to Mbare is Woods' comfortable suburban home, surrounded by well-tended gardens flanking a swimming pool, and supposedly located in East London, South Africa (these sequences were actually filmed in **Avondale**, an upscale neighborhood outside Harare city center). The massive gathering of mourners at Steve Biko's funeral was shot at the **Chibuku Stadium** in **Chitungwiza**, where political rallies and sports events are still held. In 2008 it hosted rallies for Morgan Tsvangirai, the leader of Zimbabwe's opposition party, Movement for Democratic Change, which has sought to wrest power from Robert Mugabe, head of government since 1980. Zimbabwe's second largest city, **Bulawayo**, was another stand-in for East London in the shooting of *Cry Freedom*, its "retro" look making it a perfect dub for late 1970s South Africa. Beach scenes in which Donald and Wendy Woods discuss the idea of escaping South Africa, so that Donald can expose the true story of Biko's murder by the government, were filmed in **Mombasa, Kenya**.

---

^ *Cry Freedom*, 1987. photo: ©Universal/Everett Collection
< [top] **Robben Island** photo: ©Peter Koblimiller
[bottom] **Victoria and Albert Waterfront** photo: ©Steven Allan

Films about apartheid often include at least a shot or two of **Robben Island**. Located in Table Bay, seven kilometers from Cape Town, Robben Island is the infamous prison that held, among others, South Africa's revered freedom fighter and first democratically elected president, Nelson Mandela. Actual apartheid-era footage of the prison was used in the closing scenes of *Catch A Fire*, as was new footage, shot on the island and at the **ferry landing in Cape Town's Waterfront**, in the scene where Patrick Chamusso is released.

Once known for its beautiful landscapes rather than its troubled politics and disastrous economy, **Zimbabwe** was host to the 1990 Clint Eastwood production of *White Hunter, Black Heart*. A thinly veiled account of famous American film director John Huston's time in Africa while filming *The*

African Queen, *White Hunter* made use of Zimbabwe's magnificent geography to suggest the settings of the Democratic Republic of Congo and Uganda (where much of *The African Queen* was shot). One of its most memorable scenes takes place at the fictional Lake Victoria Hotel, where Eastwood's John Wilson verbally shreds an anti-Semitic woman. The film's "Lake Victoria" is in fact **Lake Kariba**, a large man-made reservoir on the mouth of the **Zambezi River**. Wilson is an obsessed visionary, and his obsession in this film is to hunt and kill an elephant; the tragic safari scene in which he gets more than he bargained for was shot at **Hwange National Park**. Located between Bulawayo and Victoria Falls and measuring over 5,600 square miles, Hwange was once one of the continent's finest game areas, particularly well known for its huge elephant population. The film's first views of Africa were shot over the world-famous **Victoria Falls**, and the scene in which Wilson forces his irritating production assistant to "test" the seaworthiness of the craft that is meant to be the African Queen was shot on the Zambezi River—an exercise which in fact destroyed that (not seaworthy) boat.

But thanks to its multitude of stunning, varied natural locations and well-developed infrastructure, South Africa's film industry has blossomed since the fall of apartheid, and the country is now used as a stand-in for many *other* African nations in film. In the 2006 film *Blood Diamond*, the country's

Eastern Province was used as a substitute for Sierra Leone. The scenes in the Kono diamond mine were shot in a gorge along the Eastern Province's **Wild Coast**. In the film's final scenes, where Danny Archer (Leonardo DiCaprio), Solomon Vandy (Djimon Hounsou) and Solomon's son, having recovered the coveted diamond, run up a steep hill to escape some pursuing mercenaries, the fantastic surroundings are in reality **Sigidi area of Pondoland**. Home to a unique and threatened floral biodiversity that survives only in its river gorges, Pondoland's soil is also rich in minerals—recall DiCaprio clutching a handful of the red soil as he lies on a cliff—that have become a source of contention between conservationists and mining companies interested in extracting the land's titanium. Experiencing a change of heart in his last moments, DiCaprio's Archer phones love interest/journalist Maddy Bowen (Jennifer Connelly), who is lunching at **Cape Town's Victoria and Albert Waterfront**, which offers a view of one of southern Africa's most clearly recognizable landmarks: **Table Mountain**. And finally, the scene in which Danny Archer discusses retrieving the diamond with Colonel Cotezee was shot in the Western Cape, this time in the bucolic wine country around **Stellenbosch**. §

Lee Middleton has traveled and worked in 34 countries across five continents. She currently resides in Africa.

∧ *Blood Diamond*, 2006. photo: ©Warner Bros./Everett Collection
< Stellenbosch photo: ©Pichugin Dmitry
[next page] **State Library of Victoria**, Melbourne, Australia photo: ©Neale Cousland

READING / VIEWING

APPENDIX

SUGGESTED READING/VIEWING

Brodie, Ian. *Lord of the Rings Location Guidebook*. Extended Edition. Harper Collins, 2005.

O'Regan, Tom. *Australian National Cinema*. Routledge, 1996.

Reeves, Tony. *The Worldwide Guide to Movie Locations: The Ultimate Travel Guide to Film Sites Around the World*. London: Titan, 2001.

Hepburn, Katharine. *The Making of The African Queen: Or, How I Went to Africa With Bogart, Bacall and Huston and Almost Lost My Mind*. New York: Knopf, 1987.

Dineson, Isak. *Out of Africa*. New York: Vintage, 1989.

Kapsis, Robert E. & Coblentz, Kathie. *Clint Eastwood: Interviews*. Miss: UP Mississippi, 1999.

Foden, Giles. *The Last King of Scotland*. New York: Vintage, 1999.

Fossey, Dian. *Gorillas in the Mist*. New York: Houghton Mifflin, 2000.

Halsey Carr, Rosamund. *Land of a Thousand Hills: My Life in Rwanda*. New York: Penguin/Plume, 2000.

Ondaatje, Michael. *The English Patient*. New York: Vintage, 1993.

Not Quite Hollywood: The Wild, Untold Story of Ozploitation!, 2008. Directed by Mark Hartley. Madman Cinema.

Cinema of Unease, 1995 . Directors Sam Neill, Judy Rymer. BFI/Top Shelf Productions.

INDEX + CREDITS
FILM

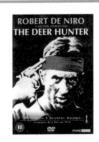

  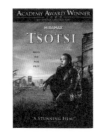 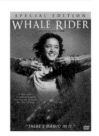

ABOUT MUSEYON GUIDES

Museyon: A Curated Guide to Your Obsessions is a guidebook series that gives the curious subject a new and differently informed look at their interests. Based out of New York City with origins in Tokyo, Paris, and just about everywhere in between, Museyon is an independent publisher of quality information.

ABOUT THE ILLUSTRATOR

 Jillian Tamaki is an illustrator from Calgary, Alberta who now lives in Brooklyn, NY. In addition to her myriad editorial illustrations for publications such as *Entertainment Weekly*, *The New York Times* and *SPIN*, she is also an award-winning graphic novelist. Co-authored with her cousin Mariko Tamaki, *Skim* was released in March 2008 and received the Ignatz Award for Best Graphic Novel.

Most memorable film/travel experience: While driving around Iceland, we got snowed in at the very top of the island, in a city called Akureyri. To while away the time, we hit the local theater which was playing the film *Stardust*, part of which happened to be filmed in Iceland. The mossy green hills were instantly recognizable and the people in the theatre were quite amused, pointing and chuckling. It was very strange to be in a movie theatre near the Arctic Circle, and even stranger to see the landscape we'd been moving through for the last week up on the screen.

ACKNOWLEDGEMENTS

Photography for the Museyon Guides has been graciously provided by dozens of citizen photographers found through Flickr.com. Museyon would like to thank them, and all the companies and photo libraries below:

Photo Editor/Contributor: Michael Kuhle

flickr: 8, 10, 12, 13, 15, 16, 22, 24, 26, 31, 31, 32, 35, 36, 40, 44, 47, 48, 54, 57, 61, 63, 68, 69, 79, 82, 84, 88, 105, 106, 132, 144, 147

istockphoto: 50, 58, 62, 68, 72, 80, 86, 98, 101, 116, 119, 124, 126, 128, 131, 140, 138, 142, 146

shutterstock: 18, 21, 28, 38, 52, 66, 71, 75, 76, 90, 94, 96, 131, 135, 150, 102, 108, 110, 112, 115, 120, 136

Everett Collection: 11, 14, 23, 27, 30, 41, 49, 53, 60, 67, 77, 91, 99, 104, 113, 127, 133, 143

Every effort has been made to trace and compensate copyright holders, and we apologize in advance for any accidental omissions. We would be happy to apply the corrections in the following editions of this publication.